I'

SAID THAT

I WISH I'D
SAID THAT

Right words spoken result
in changed behavior and
open new opportunities.

James Rennell, DMin
& Jann Cupp, PhD

TATE PUBLISHING & Enterprises

Published by Tate Publishing & Enterprises, LLC
127 E. Trade Center Terrace | Mustang, Oklahoma 73064 USA
1.888.361.9473 | www.tatepublishing.com

Tate Publishing is committed to excellence in the publishing industry. The company reflects the philosophy established by the founders, based on Psalm 68:11,
"The Lord gave the word and great was the company of those who published it."

Book design copyright © 2008 by Tate Publishing, LLC. All rights reserved.
Cover design by Janae Glass
Interior design by Kandi Evans

Published in the United States of America

ISBN: 978-1-60604-483-4
1. Biblical Studies: Old Testament: Writings and Wisdom
2. Christian Living: Practical Life: Personal Growth/Communication
08.06.20

DEDICATION

How do you say thank you to the hundreds of teachers, authors, professors, fellow ministers, friends, and family who have shared their work and lives with you over the years? These chapters are really about them. It is your stories and interactions with others and me that make these pages true and personal. To you who nurtured, shared, and helped me, I dedicate this book.

—Jim Rennell

ACKNOWLEDGMENTS

This book has been over forty years in the making. As an associate in the Sunday school department of the Kentucky Baptist Convention back in 1977, one of the goals I set for myself was to write a book about how important words are in ministry. Now after a thirty-year military career and a couple of other retirements, I decided it was time to start.

For this book I owe a great debt to those whose names and works have found their way into my ministry and illustration file. It all started back in 1959 when I began to speak in small churches near the Fort Campbell military base where I was stationed. An army friend, Jim Pollard, mentioned to his father, who was the state Sunday school director for the Louisiana Baptist Convention, about my opportunities. His father sent a thick folder of illustrations, outlines, and ideas to help me begin my ministry. In those early years, before I learned the importance of crediting speakers, authors, and writers for their work, I simply cut, copied, pasted, and filed stories, illustrations, and bulletin notes in folders. As the years passed, I pasted, typed, and filed this information on 20,000+ 3x5 cards by topic. In that process I sometimes eliminated dates, authors, and sources, so the information would fit on the 3x5 cards. I regret that some illustrations I heard from speakers and friends made their way into the file without a source or date. Please accept my apology if something in my words and ideas here sound familiar to yours.

—Jim Rennell

TABLE OF CONTENTS

FOREWORD

The authors have written a book that will appeal to people on several levels. For members of the clergy, it offers a wealth of information that will be useful in preparing homilies. For the layperson, it presents vivid examples of how words have power to change lives.

When reading an early draft of this book four questions came to mind:

1. Have the authors written a cogent narrative of selected Old Testament events that demonstrate the power of words?

2. Have the authors shown how people in those biblical times responded, for good or ill, to these events?

3. Have the authors shown how these responses could be applied to events in our modern day lives?

4. Have the authors presented a primer for helping us lead an ethical and happy life where we not only do things right, we also do the right things?

I believe the answers to these questions are yes, yes, yes, and yes. In these times when it is becoming increasingly difficult to find leaders or role-models who have accurate moral compasses, this book presents an excellent guide to how our responses to the principles presented here will help us to lead the good and ethical life.

The authors have shown how words have power to change lives not only in the Old Testament but also in our everyday lives. They have also written a narrative that has led me to say at many points in reading their own words: I wish I'd said That.

Dr. Angelo A. Volpe
President Emeritus
Tennessee Technological University

INTRODUCTION

WORDS, WHAT WOULD WE DO WITHOUT THEM?

Words are what we live and die by. Words compel us to action and change our behavior. With words we exercise our faith, commit our love, destroy our enemies, and practice nation building. We evaluate people and events with the words that are used about them. To quote Aldus Huxley, "the function of language is two-fold: to communicate emotion and to give information" (Public Radio, 2007). Our words put into language makes us human. All this reminds me of the time a church leader once said, "It seems strange to me if we get a preacher who can preach the right words, he can't do anything else, and if we get one that can do all the right stuff, he can't preach. Why can't we find one who can do both?" Right words and right actions in the same person are not necessarily a rare combination. With a little effort and forethought, most of us could be a person who practices what we preach.

My church leader's evaluation of preachers probably included me. His thoughts are certainly open to a variety of interpretations. What he felt were shortcomings in his pastor others might praise as gifts. The same can be said about most communication. For example, take any national or religious debate. Sometimes the debaters are poles apart. Sometimes they are saying the same thing only using different words. To add to the confusion, media and political pundits offer a different spin on the debaters' words or actions, adding one more interpretation to the debate. Who is right? What are we to believe as truth? When is it time to commit our lives, resources, and actions? My father often cautioned me when I would get all hyped up about what someone said or did with these words: "Is this the battle you are ready to die for? If not, then maybe you need to think about some other solution besides getting angry."

Psychiatrist Dr. William Glasser, founder of *Reality Therapy,* said in a seminar I attended, "no one ever makes a wrong decision" (1965). Those few words really caught my attention. I sat up and listened. *Surely,* I thought, *he was wrong about that!* Then he went on to explain. "In their own mind everyone believes that what they are saying or doing is right or else they wouldn't say it or do it" (Glasser, 1974). The more that I thought about this, the more I realized *he was right.* What people say and do always seems right for them even though many observers and listeners will have different opinions. Words can be and are powerful motivators, compelling us to act positively or negatively depending on our perception of what those words mean. Guy Deutscher said it correctly in his book, *The Unfolding of Language,* "Everyone knows that the words of a language, from its aardvarks to its zucchini, lend meaning to our utterances and allow us to understand one another" (2005).

Even words found in scripture do not escape changes in meaning over time or the fiery rhetoric of well-meaning preachers and Bible scholars. I remember a heated debate in seminary when Clarence Jordan came out with his *Cotton Patch* translation of the Bible. There were those who felt he should have been awarded the Nobel Prize for peace and/or literature and those who were sure his work was a ticket to damnation for anyone who read his words or followed his work. Scripture easily falls into a category that subjects it to different interpretations, points of view, and perceptions. And yet, scripture has had an impact on our world like no other written document. How can it have such an impact for good and still cause such great confusion, anger, and hatred…even among men and women within the same religious group who confess Jesus as their Lord? Army Colonel Dick Hallock, in my view, said it right, "Words are bullets and should be used sparingly, aimed toward a target" (2007).

My own view is that scripture has little meaning (right words for us) until we are willing to make its application (right actions) to our own lives. Language is more than words. The meanings we give words make up our conversations, build our relationships, and establish our morals and values. This means because we interpret words differently, we will not all react to the same written words in scripture, but to the interpretation we give to those words based on our own experience. Therefore, when these simple stories and words take on meaning for us, they become forces that change our behavior. Short Bible stories, sometimes shorter than a few hundred words, can have a greater impact on a person's future than earning a college degree or acquiring fame and wealth.

New and exciting research into human behavior and how the brain processes information can help us understand how words lead us into behavioral changes. Collaborating with Dr. Jann Cupp, professor of counseling and psychology at Tennessee Technological University, for this book has been an exciting experience for both of us. His contributions help the reader understand more about how the mind works and what motivates us to use words in an attempt to influence people to make significant lifestyle changes.

In the following chapters, I have tried to use fifteen simple events from the Old Testament under the title *I Wish I'd Said That* and show how a few words changed someone's life, turned circumstances around for the better, or gave new meaning and insight for a new solution to a complex problem. If the process worked in these Bible stories, why can't the same process work for us today as ministers, teachers, counselors, and parents? Please forgive me if as you read these chapters you believe I have taken too much liberty and license, or missed the obvious in emphasizing the minutia. My goal is to point out the power of Bible words that changed lives. The stories I have chosen, in my opinion, do that. Maybe Dr. Glasser is correct; in our minds we all may believe our perception is the right one. But it is our faith response to these words and stories that make us come out with different actions and behaviors. The title, *I Wish I'd Said That,* is an idea most of us have considered. Hopefully, these chapters will lead you to think carefully for the right words that will make a difference for someone and change his or her life for good.

Dr. Jim Rennell
Cookeville, Tennessee

Words of Compassion and Bravery

ELI SAID TO SAMUEL...

"GO BACK TO BED."

1 SAMUEL 3:9

FIND A PLACE WHERE DECISIONS CAN BE MADE.

There have been very few times in my life when I appreciated someone telling me that I should go to bed just because they said so. It seems to me that going to bed should be a decision I make on my own without help from a parent, spouse, or friend. But life is not always lived as we desire. Take, for example, this confusing conversation between the young child, Samuel, and Eli, the old priest, in 1 Samuel 3. Young Samuel thinks Eli has called him from his bed to come into his room, but the old priest replies, "No, I didn't call you, go back to bed." The boy obeys, goes back to bed, but he does not stay there for long. This night, that still small voice will call two more times, and Samuel's life, as well as the old priest's, will be changed forever.

Generally, it takes only a few well-chosen words in a difficult situation to transform our attitude or perception and give us a new or different point of view. The right words, spoken at the right time, provide us with the motivation and courage needed to carry us successfully through a difficult time to a new calling or place of ministry. But who will speak those "right words"? And how much will those words influence the moment or circumstance? In addition, we all know that sometimes it is our silence or what is not said that changes an unpleasant moment into a pleasant one.

The older I get the less likely I am to listen and appreciate someone's words telling me what I need to do. Call it male ego or stubbornness; I like to think that I am mature enough to make up my own mind about my life and work. Certainly I am wrong about that. When I reach an impasse, I must suppress my ego and ask for help. No matter how hard I want to believe at my age, 70+, that I do not need someone else to help, I still do. Samuel's situation was a little different. He was a child and thought he understood Eli's voice and responded in the only way he knew, by getting up and saying, "You called me?" The circumstances became more confusing when Samuel was told on all three occasions he was mistaken. On the first two occasions the old priest Eli also might have passed it off as a child's misunderstanding. But on the third occasion

Samuel's few words, "Surely you did call me," triggered Eli's mind to start searching for a solution to the child's dilemma. His counsel to young Samuel on the third trip back to his bedside would not bring the old priest comfort. Eli remembered his own call and may have wondered, *Could the Lord be calling Samuel to replace me?* Wisely, Eli spoke, "Go back to bed, but this time when you hear the voice say these words" (1 Samuel 3:9, nasb). Young Samuel did as he was told, and from that moment on, his life and work were changed.

I am writing this chapter during Super Bowl weekend. One team huddles to consider their next play. The coach sends in a new play or player, and then the quarterback says a few simple words so his team will understand, such as "pass 41, right out on 2, Jack stay back and block." A few words, executed correctly, give the team that big play that makes a touchdown. However you do not have to play in a Super Bowl to hear a few words that can make you successful. A few simple words rightly understood and obeyed, like those spoken to Samuel, can come to you in the night and change your life forever.

First Samuel 3 tells us that young Samuel slept in the room where the Ark of the Covenant was kept, just like he had so many nights before. Eli slept in a nearby room. It was early evening. Scripture tells us, "The lamp of God had not yet gone out" (1 Samuel 3:3, nasb). Lamps back then were simple pottery dishes pinched at one end with a wick that reached down into olive oil in the bottom of the dish. When the oil burned away during the night, the lamp went out (Funk and Ben-Dor, 1962).

Eli, the priest, was old and may have wondered if his death was near. He had gone to his room for the night. Like Samuel, he assumed this night would be like most other nights. He would lie down on his pallet over a bed of straw and cover or wrap himself in his blanket and sleep. If he were well and not sick or bothered, he would rest and strengthen himself for the next repetitious day as temple priest. But it would not be so on this night. This night would number his days. On this night in the Shiloh sanctuary, God's voice would call a new young prophet. Everything was about to change. Eli's few words and Samuel's obedient response would change Israel's future. Samuel would take Eli's place and lead Israel in a different direction.

Samuel's age may have been as young as eight to ten years old. His day was usually filled with running errands for Eli: filling lamps with oil, cleaning and preparing the temple for the Lord's business. Nighttime came as a welcome respite. It was a time to relax and think a little about which words and events provided him with some new information about life and his future. Both Eli and Samuel assumed this night would be like other nights. In a few minutes, their tired bodies would merge into a deep sleep until morning brought another day.

Eli plays the parent's role in this passage. There

were times when I was a child that my parents would say to me if it were bedtime or I was sick or troublesome, "It's time for you to go to bed." It seemed to me these few words were always their solution to any situation. But, with four boys at home, sending one or all of them to bed provided my parents with a few noise-free minutes when they could talk, read, or just enjoy the quiet. Even today this is still not an uncommon approach for a parent to take with noisy or troublesome children.

This night would be one of those times all parents with children experience. Things are quiet, sleep is a few seconds away, and then a child's voice breaks the stillness, "I want a glass of water." Or your child comes and stands beside your bed saying sorrowfully, "I can't sleep." Acceptable and unacceptable options go through a parent's mind as how best to handle the child's dilemma. Samuel lies down to sleep, then hears what he believes is Eli's voice. He gets up and goes into Eli's room saying, "Here I am, you called me?" Eli replies, "I did not call you, go back and lie down" (1 Samuel 3:5, nasb). Samuel returns to bed confused, but obedient. Children often misunderstand adult conversation because their experience and information storage is not as great as that of adults; therefore they misinterpret or cannot grasp the concepts common and familiar to adults.

Scripture tells us that Samuel was young and did not know the Lord. When Samuel hears the voice for a third time, he treks down to Eli's room again. Now the old priest suspects there is more to this situation than a child's inability to sleep. In his mind he reasons maybe the Lord is involved here. So he instructs young Samuel with these simple words, "Go lie down, and it shall be if He calls you, that you shall say, 'Speak, Lord, for Thy servant is listening'" (1 Samuel 3:9, nasb). There are lots of reasons for sending a child back to bed, just as there are reasons for an adult to go to bed. When I am tired, stressed-out from my work, or ill, I return to an old familiar routine. I take a hot bath, drink a glass of water, and go to bed. Fortunately for me sleep usually comes quickly, and after a good night's sleep, I feel more like facing yesterday's problems the next morning. "Go to bed" may sound childish, and it may not be good medical advice for everyone, but it works for me. Eight hours' sleep does wonders for my mind and body and sets my worries aside for a while. I do not view going to bed early as hiding or running away from my problems. Quite the contrary, it comes as a respite, a quiet time, a time away from the noise and the crowd. It is a time for renewing mind and body.

Experts are torn on whether sleep primarily serves the body or the mind. Our own experience tells us that it certainly serves both. Some researchers have proposed that there exists a "core sleep," where the heavy-duty restoration of mind takes place, followed by "optional sleep," which fills the rest of our sleep time and allows the cells of our bodies to be restored by the circulatory system (Horne, 1988). This could explain why we often feel rested after a brief nap. Sleep studies have also shown that the perception of being rested and renewed occurs more in relation to stage one or REM (Rapid Eye Movement) sleep than any other level. REM sleep is the light, almost awake sleep time when our most vivid dreams occur (Lefton, 2000). Many of these studies indicate that loss of this specific phase of sleep leaves us agitated and irritable, and gets us "up on the wrong side of the bed" (Kecklund, Akerstedt & Lowden, 1997).

Sleep is good for the mind and the body. But there is a third benefit that comes to most of us: we do a little problem solving. Yesterday's stress may have dulled your creativity and hidden your problem-solving tools. During the night your mind subconsciously worked on the problem, and the next morning, suddenly, you have a solution. Sometimes stress denies us the focus and energy we need to do our best work and make better choices. Have you ever said, "I am worn out! I wish I could just go home and go to bed for a while"? You know from experience that a good night's rest can clear the mind. So whether it is for resting the body, clearing the mind, or waiting for the Lord to speak in the still of the night, your bed is the place where your future may be decided.

Usually nighttime brings a few minutes to meditate, reflect, and think about the day's events. It is a time to open our mind and listen for the Lord to speak.

Listening and thinking puts us on the right track for God's spirit to bring us words of wisdom. There certainly is biblical evidence where God's voice came and spoke to people in their dreams and sleep. I believe that history will never be able to record all the thoughts and conversations people have had with the Lord from their bed. Whether it is your habit to close the day with prayer or have a quiet meditation, nighttime is for many of us our spiritual quiet time. It is a time to talk to the Lord and let the Lord talk to us.

In my early ministry, I had a pastor friend tell me that God called him just as he called Samuel, three times in the night. His life and ministry reflected his response to that night when God called him. He is not the only person who found God's voice calling him while he rested in the bedroom. It was that same gentle voice that spoke to Elijah after he fled from Jezebel's wrath. And that voice spoke to Joseph in a dream telling him to take the child Jesus and flee to Egypt. God's voice still speaks today if we are in a place where we can hear it. Some nights and dreams may turn out fearful. God came to Abimelech in a dream one night and said to him, "You are as good as dead because of the woman you have taken; she is a married woman" (Genesis 20:3, nasb). His dream changed his plans about taking another wife. Dreams that become nightmares are not uncommon. There are nights, however, when our dreams become life changing or instructive and we are changed forever. Christianity moved into Europe during one of those nights when the Apostle Paul had a vision of a man of Macedonia standing and begging him, "Come over to Macedonia and help us" (Acts 16:9, nasb).

Most cognitive psychologists agree that sleep is the time our minds use to organize data from our day. Subsequently, dreams are the byproduct of our mind's filing system. As we sleep, we move files around, mull over thoughts, attempt to label concepts, and link them to already existing memories. As a result, we experience dreams. Our dreams usually involve something encountered during the day—though it may be highly symbolic (Carpenter, 2001). The thought or concept may get linked to an old memory and become quite bizarre. Nonetheless, it is our mind putting its house in order. We are simply witnesses, watching the pictures go by (Foulkes, 1996). Recent research suggests that sleep is particularly helpful in the sorting and filing of newly learned information. In our rested state, we are able to automatically associate our new memories with those already ingrained and place them into long-term memory (Gais & Born, 2004; Huber et al., 2004).

Where can you go to find those moments with the Lord when his instructions and guidance will make a difference? I do not recommend that you regularly use your resting time for an agonizing struggle within your soul to solve all of life's problems, even though it is true that many great decisions have been made on a bed of discontent and struggle. Yes! God can talk to faithful servants anytime or at any place. It just seems that we listen better when we are separated from the crowd, listening for that still small voice that can guide our words and actions. In a familiar place, the right words can come to motivate us toward the right actions.

Go to bed and dream of opportunity. Dream the dreams where God challenges your soul to move from darkness and depression into his marvelous light. Go to bed and ask for God's spirit to come and overshadow you with his rest and peace. Go to bed and listen for that still, small voice to speak like no other voice to help you organize your thoughts, challenge your heart and soul, and move you to respond. Go to bed and ask for forgiveness while you forgive those who have hurt you. Philosopher Hannah Arendt said it best, "Forgiveness is the key to action and freedom" (Arendt, 2006). Try it! You may discover a habit that enhances your spirit as well as your mind and body. Eli said, "It shall be if he calls you, that you shall say, 'Speak Lord for thy servant is listening'" (1 Samuel 3:9, kjv). Eli's words were action words that changed a confusing night into a call to serve. Action words well chosen and spoken can make a difference for someone struggling with difficult decisions and circumstances. Your action words, carefully spoken, can make the difference. Eli said to Samuel, "Go back to bed," and he did…the rest is history. Going back to bed is not all bad. When my chance comes to say the right words, I hope I say them as wisely as Eli did.

For Further Bible Study

1. Use the concordance in the back of your Bible and look up the word *dream(s)*. See if you can find three Old Testament characters that had problems with interpreting and/or understanding their own dreams.

2. Sometimes dreams change people's lives. Can you find in Genesis three Old Testament characters whose dream(s) changed behaviors or careers?

3. Sometimes other people are needed to help us understand our dreams, scripture, and doctrine. Who helped Pharaoh interpret his dream? What couple in the New Testament helped Apollos interpret scripture correctly?

For Personal Growth

1. Recall a time when you had a conversation with a child and they did not understand the directions or information you were giving them. Review one such experience in your mind. Did you assume too much? Did they not have enough experience to carry out your request? What did you learn from this?

2. Solving problems plays an important role in every adult's daily life. Eli solved the problem for Samuel.

How would you have solved this dilemma for a young Samuel today?

3. How good are your listening skills? Do you really listen to what someone is saying to you or are you thinking about what you are going to say when he or she finishes speaking? Your library or bookstore may have several good books to help you develop better listening skills.

DAVID SAID TO SAUL...

"I WILL GO."

1 SAMUEL 17:32

THE BRAVE SELDOM SEE THE RISKS.

Everyone loves a story where good triumphs over evil. All the characteristics for a compelling story are here in this passage: plot, intrigue, courage, risk, and danger, to name only a few. History is filled with tragic and desperate moments when people stand paralyzed, afraid, not knowing what to do. Then suddenly someone will make a decision; he or she acts bravely and challenges the moment. An airplane taking off from Washington International airport crashes into the Potomac River. People start to gather and wonder what to do. A passenger emerges up out of the cold, icy water. A young man on a bridge is watching. He takes off his jacket, jumps into the water and rescues the passenger. When it is all over, some must have wondered why the young man risked his own life to rescue the passenger. Was he sure he could overcome the icy water to make the rescue, or did he not even think about it? Was he trained in water rescue? These and other questions challenge us to want to dig deeper into the story for more information. What words or events mobilize some people and not others to take it upon themselves to do something rather than wait for someone else to do something?

The main characters in this story are Saul, king of Israel; Goliath, a giant Philistine from Gath; and David, a young shepherd from Bethlehem sent by his father with food for his soldier brothers. A careful look at the characters' words and actions reveals that there are many conflicts in this passage. Many of us would like to know more about why the young boy David, who was not a warrior, was willing to risk his life fighting against a giant when hundreds of battle-experienced Israelite men and their king stood by unwilling to fight. Scripture tells us Saul also was a giant of a man, standing "head and shoulders above the rest" (1 Samuel 10:23, author's paraphrase). Why didn't he go out into battle against Goliath? Why was he so willing to let an inexperienced young man fight a giant? Samuel once said to Saul, "The Lord has torn the kingdom of Israel from you today, and has given it to your neighbor who is better than you" (1 Samuel 15:28, nasb). Was Saul afraid because Samuel told him God was rejecting him because he failed to destroy all of the Amalekites? There certainly is a possibility that Saul may have found out that Samuel had anointed David. It would be hard to keep something like that a secret. Was this Saul's way of innocently dealing with a usurper to his kingship? While many Bible readers like the story's happy ending, others crave more information about the people and events that led up to that moment when David risks his life defending Israel's God. Did Saul consider what would happen if David lost? This story is filled with intriguing issues and questions that are not answered to every Bible scholar's satisfaction.

An impulsive person is someone who is easily moved to action. David asks, "Who is this uncircumcised Philistine, that he should taunt the armies of the living God!" (1 Samuel 17:26, nasb). Was young David impulsive, tricked, or suckered into this challenge? Did Goliath's taunting convince him something must be done? Literature is filled with hundreds of historical stories where some huge warrior or darkly dressed villain challenges a smaller or unknown person to come up and whip him. When David asks why someone from Saul's army doesn't respond to Goliath's challenge, he discovers his honest words ignited his brother's anger. Eliab is impulsive and explodes with words that do not directly answer David's question. He chastens David for leaving his father's sheep in the field to come down and watch the battle. The great psychiatrist Carl Jung said, "Everything that irritates us about others can lead us to an understanding of ourselves" (Jung, 2006). Did Eliab's words anger David to act impulsively? Was

David thinking, *I'll show you I am not the wimp you think I am!?* Impulsiveness is not always a valued trait, for many have found themselves in deeper difficulties because they failed to think things through before jumping into a quick decision to act. What young man is not interested in watching a fight? There is something about grown men in mortal combat that draws a crowd. Hollywood has made millions of dollars by pitting two men with dueling pistols trying to prove which one is faster, tougher, or wiser. Sometimes men may fight to win a lady's favor or hand in marriage. Is this a consideration? Apparently, Saul made such an offer, for the soldiers tell David, "…the king will enrich the man who kills him (Goliath) with riches and will give him his daughter and make his father's house free in Israel" (1 Samuel 17:25, n a s b). Will David's curiosity and the opportunity to win the king's daughter tempt him enough to go into mortal combat? Is Goliath's "winner takes all" view reason enough for the challenge?

Reading further we discover that David perceives the situation quite differently. His interest in this battle is more than mere curiosity, impulsiveness, or the king's daughter. He sees the battle as defending the honor of Israel's God. David knows he is God's anointed. Does this situation call for him to step forward and demonstrate that he is God's chosen? I doubt his concern is to test God or himself. David's bravery had already been tested when he was a shepherd. He tells Saul how he defended his father's flock against a lion and a bear. "The Lord who delivered me from the jaw of the lion and the paw of the bear; He will deliver me from the hand of the Philistine" (1 Samuel 17:37, nasb). Many Bible leaders and warriors were motivated by a faith or belief that they were God's designated and anointed servant. Was David convinced that this was the moment he was anointed for? A careful reading of these passages indicates there seems to be little doubt in David's mind that he was prepared to take on the giant Goliath if God was ready for him to do battle against this enemy. The Bible gives us a host of men and women who stood up and defended Israel against her enemies: Joshua, Jael, Gideon, and Jehu, to name only a few.

David understood Goliath's words as a taunt against Israel and an insult to Jehovah God. He hears these verbal barbs as his call to defend the Lord's honor and save Israel. Great leaders have an intuitive feeling or gift that allows them to sense when the moment calls and beckons for them to step forward. Some are self-disciplined; others more serendipitous. Always sensing the big picture, they are hungry for information that will provide them with the opportunity and right moment to act. They can trust their own intuition. This helps them to see beyond the moment to view themselves in the winner's circle. David may have seen Goliath's taunt as a new beginning and understood that the Lord had prepared him for this moment. When he looked beyond the battle with Goliath to a future moment, did he see himself as God's new chosen leader for Israel? He would not pass up this opportunity to fulfill his destiny as Israel's future king. Goliath's words were David's challenge for action.

One of the first things I notice here is that David's motivation comes from the same high moral and ethical standard God sets for his people every day. The right behavior calls for the righteousness of the cause as the correct stimulus for action. Today, the idea of a high moral and ethical behavior is not readily found on athletic playing fields, in corporate boardrooms, or in government chambers. Many leaders in business, sports programs, and politics, as well as pastors and lay leaders believe that high moral and ethical standards are unimportant when seeking high offices or taking advantage of an opportunity for greatness. When this happens, it is easy to see that sometimes their real values are found in salary packages and benefits that are exorbitant and unnecessary. Today we read about chief financial officers who have no problem with making phony financial reports to their boards, the public, and the government. And what about the athletes who use illegal drugs and steroids, or basketball referees accepting bribes and payoffs? Are these acceptable marketplace and business practices? The prevailing attitude is *what is in it for me?* Such a mind-set lacks the spiritual discipline that calls for an understanding that doing things God's way is more important than money and power. What hope is there for an organization when some Christian leaders act as monarchs over a kingdom instead of serving those they were elected or chosen to shepherd? Should we not blush when some Christians abuse their wealth and resources with the excuse that they are too busy to serve God? What should we think when Christian leaders sport huge diamond rings, designer clothes, and live in mansions and vacation homes built and purchased with donations given by people who believed their gifts were going to be used for ministry and not personal opulence? The highest moral values are always the right standard required for those who desire to lead God's people. David put his God and the needs of others before himself in this battle with Goliath.

Secondly, great leaders have a vision. If Israel is to be the nation God intends them to be, then this battle with the Philistines must end here with a victory. Israel's future as a nation begins with the defeat of Goliath. This young man brings to this event what Israel's army didn't have in Saul or themselves, a vision and willingness to follow God's leadership regardless of the dangers, risks, or cost. Goliath's words motivated David's behavior. Young David challenged the nation to take a stand against her enemies starting now with Goliath. As a result of Goliath's defeat, when Saul and David return from another battle, the women sang, "Saul has slain his thousands and David his ten thousands" (1 Samuel 18:7, nasb). The right words and actions replaced Saul's unblessed leadership and a standing army unwilling to defend God's honor. "Where there is no vision, the people perish..." (Proverbs 29:18, kjv).

Next, I think all leaders and warriors have a high sense of self-confidence and a belief in self-efficacy. Their confidence that they will succeed is directly linked to actual success. Renowned cognitive psychologist Albert Bandura demonstrated this time after time in his own research into what he calls "reciprocal determinism" (Bandura, 1978). Leaders with a high belief in their own success are more likely to accept challenges, improve their performance, and succeed (Harris & Halpin, 2002; Bandura, 1997). How you think about succeeding can lead to success. This is an idea that is being applied more and more by organizations and businesses. Modern athletes are more frequently hiring sports psychologists to help them visualize winning in order to increase confidence and self-efficacy and consequently, their chances of winning (Murphy, 1990; Jaffe, 2004). Health care professionals help patients find healing and wholeness through the use of guided imagery (Smith, 2000).

David's self-confidence motivates his mind to action. Determined and brave, using his crude sling and few stones, he seeks the right moment to strike. His inspiration for a victory for God's people drives him forward into the valley, ready for battle. He is so confident that he rejects Saul's armor as too heavy and untested. There is an old saying that applies here. "It is not the size of the dog in the fight that counts, but the size of the fight in the dog that makes the difference." David had a fire in his belly to defeat the giant. Goliath's overconfidence and bluster became the stumbling blocks that took him down to defeat. His weapons, huge size, and a bully's reputation would not serve him well in this battle. David's humble trust in the Lord and simple weapons gave him the victory. The new buzzword today is "social identity." It is the belief that leaders can best represent that identity that they "…will have the most influence over the group's members…" (Reicher, Haslam & Platow, 2007).

I cannot help but wonder when our own self-confidence becomes overconfidence. We do not start out in life overconfident. As children we often need to be encouraged with words like, "Try again and you'll get it right next time." Then somewhere in our late teens or early adulthood we get the idea after a few successes we think we can do no wrong. Most of us with the right stimulation can go from a little confidence to overconfidence in a matter of minutes. People are willing to forgive our mistakes when they do not come from overindulgence, overconfidence, and abuse of power. David's self-confidence turned from a shepherd defending his God against a giant to a king filled with lust, desire, and overconfidence in his conquest for Bathsheba. God sent Nathan, the prophet, to point out David's sin and shortcomings. Today we tend to gloss over our national and corporate leaders with excuses that others have done the same things in the past only we didn't know it until they were deceased. I don't know about you, but I grow tired hearing about our political leaders' mistakes that are somehow justified because some leader generations years ago did the same thing and got away with it. Sin is sin, wrong is wrong, no matter if it is committed in the past or present. Sin wasn't right for them then; it isn't right for others now. All of us are accountable to the Lord for our words and actions. David has the right motives for the right mission.

What kind of leadership do you want for your nation, community, and home? Before deciding on what path or course of action to take there are issues that need to be settled in your own heart and mind. Who are you? Why should you respond to a call for leadership when an opportunity becomes available? What does this work have to do with God's plan for your life? David knew who he was and understood clearly God's call for the moment. The valley between the mountains and the upcoming battle with Goliath came after he first knew himself. There is a tremendous difference between those whom God has called and chosen and those who, because of their own ego and ambition, want the rewards that go with leadership and victory. Not all who claim God's call are worthy of the opportunity to lead his people. Israel was on a downhill slide under Saul's failing leadership. The Lord sent a new leader. Churches and religious organizations can find themselves in the same valley of decision today. Does this person under consideration for leadership have that social identity, spiritual and moral values to lead God's people, or are they too overconfident in their skills and abilities. Watch out for prospective leaders whose words and actions build kingdoms for themselves under the guise of caring for others and conducting God's business.

In Isaiah 6:8 we read, "Whom shall I send, and who will go for us? Then I said, 'Here am I. Send me!'" (nasb). God's call in Isaiah is no different from God's call to Jeremiah, David, you, or me. Young David stood before King Saul saying, "Let no man's heart fail on account of him; your servant will go and fight with this Philistine," and he did (1 Samuel 17:32, nasb). Standing on that hillside that day when Goliath issued his challenge were many experienced Israelite warriors. When the soldiers heard his taunts and threat "they were dismayed and greatly afraid" (1 Samuel 17:11, nasb). When David's brothers looked out into the valley, they saw a huge obstacle named Goliath baring their way to success, their hearts melted. The giant's size immobilized Israel's warriors from starting. The giant and the facts surrounding this moment couldn't keep David out of the fight in the valley. It is foolish to fight battles God has not called us to wage. And it is just as foolish to stand by weak-kneed and faint-hearted and allow what God has provided to be taken away by evil men. David saw what Saul, his brothers, and the other men of Israel failed to see and said, "Let no man's heart fail on account of him, your servant will go and fight with this Philistine" (1 Samuel 17:32, nasb). Are we listening for that still, small voice calling us to stand and fight, or are we listening to our own weak hearts telling us to walk away? How we interpret the words of our call will determine what action we take.

For Further Bible Study

1. Who were some other great men in the Old Testament that slew a giant?

2. What tools did Gideon use to create fear in the Midian army?

3. What animal did Goliath compare himself to when he saw young David coming out to fight against him?

For Personal Growth

1. Who is someone that you consider courageous? Why? Does this person have integrity because of what they say or do? What would you look for to find integrity if they had both?

2. The slingshot is not a weapon used today against bullies. What are some spiritual tools that are acceptable to use against those who bully others?

3. What Internet suggestions can you find that are

alternatives to wars and differences between individuals and/or nations?

ELDERS SAID TO REHOBOAM...

"THEY WILL BE YOUR SERVANTS."

1 KINGS 12:1–17

THE WISE THINK BEFORE THEY SPEAK.

Has anyone ever tried to program you to give a specific answer? Most of us have experienced this uncomfortable feeling. Salespeople are often taught to make their presentation in such a way that when they finish, the only correct answer is for the listener to say, "Yes," and then purchase the product or service. Programming people can be dangerous because it causes people to reject their own logic and critical thinking skills and trade them for deliberately unintended or overly simplistic solutions. Parents often use a similar type of programming for raising children. They repeat their guidance to children over and over until the child will say or do what the parents wanted them to do. "Tell Mommy you are sorry for spilling your milk on the floor." Dutifully, the child says, "I am sorry, Mommy" and learns what words and actions are proper when future accidents occur. A young couple was using this kind of child psychology to train their daughter for bedtime. Mom said, "It is time for bed, Ellen, would you like to take your stuffed teddy bear or bunny with you to bed tonight?" No matter which stuffed animal the child chose, the next step was to put her to bed. One evening as bedtime approached little Ellen said, "Before I go to bed, do you want me to watch cartoons on TV or play with my toys in the den?" Suddenly this became a teachable moment for Ellen's parents about who is training whom.

Programming people to give the right answer is really not a new strategy. This was a tactic used ages ago. Jeroboam, son of Nebat, disagreed with King Solomon's rules and had to flee to Egypt. When he heard that Solomon was dead, he returned to his home in Canaan. After his return, Rehoboam, Solomon's son and heir, sent for him. Jeroboam represented the ten northern tribes in Israel when he said, "Your father put a heavy yoke on us, but now lighten the harsh labor and the heavy yoke he put on us, and we will serve you" (1 Kings 12:4, nasb). He tried to program King Rehoboam to say, "Yes, I will lighten your load." But Rehoboam answered, "Come back to me in three days." King Rehoboam consulted the elders who had served his father, Solomon, during his lifetime. "How would you advise me to answer these people?" he asked (1

Kings 12:6, nasb). The elders replied, "If you will be kind to these people and please them and give them a favorable answer, they will always be your servants forever" (1 Kings 12:7, nasb). Almost without thinking, Rehoboam rejected the elders' wisdom and counsel and consulted with his young male friends, those that had grown up with him in the court, how he should handle this situation. Their response was closer to what he wanted to hear. The younger men's advice was, "My father made your yoke heavy; I will make it even heavier. My father scourged you with whips; I will scourge you with scorpions" (1 Kings 12:11, nasb). Such words moved the question from consultation and consensus to an insulting and degrading conflict.

I served with an army commander who used the same get-tough attitude the young men suggested. His leadership philosophy was "If you start out tough, you can always loosen up later, but if you start out loose, you can never get your leadership back once you have lost it." Such an attitude sets the stage for using strong words with the hope you can program your listener to provide the behavior what you demand. In the commander's case, good men and women left the unit for another assignment.

Rehoboam accepted the younger men's advice and discovered their words soon led to a civil war that divided his kingdom in 931 BCE. The ten tribes of the north formed the nation of Israel, leaving Judah and Benjamin in the south to form the nation of Judah. Rehoboam's decision to follow his friend's advice launched the downfall and the destruction of both nations. The glory and unity that once was with David and Solomon's empires was considerably weakened. First the northern kingdom of Israel fell to the Assyrians in 724 BCE, and then Judah's kingdom would fall to Babylon in 586 BCE. There were too few great leaders and too many mediocre and weak leaders in the interim. The downfall began with Rehoboam's decision to listen to his friends. There are leaders who seem destined to ascend the throne and become successful and others whose ascension brings hardship, death, and destruction. What makes the difference? Why will some armies follow their leader's words to the ends of the earth while other leaders using the same words cause their army to rebel? Our own generation is replete with examples of dictators and tyrants, like Rehoboam, whose wrong words and actions led to their own destruction and/or destruction of their nation.

One reason why some leaders' words are accepted or rejected comes from their experience and/or the environment in which they were raised. Rehoboam watched as Solomon's kingdom grew at a rapid pace. In order to sustain the nation's growth, Solomon had to tax and conscripts his people to provide for the expanding government. Rehoboam's experience came from the top of the economic spectrum. He lived in the palace, ate at the king's table, and associated with rich senior government officials' sons and daughters. These events gave him the view that those who lived at the top of the political, economic, and social systems made the rules; citizens and slaves at the bottom obeyed them. Jeroboam's experience with Solomon's government was different. His family's life and surroundings were filled with suffering and hardship. Out of those past hardships, Jeroboam expected changes to be made if his people were to serve the new king.

It has been said that wisdom comes from experience, but then, so does failure and imprudence. Rehoboam's decision to add hardship, labor, and suffering to the ten northern tribes was an expensive and costly lesson to learn. He had other choices he could have made, but his ego and inexperience led him to make the wrong decision. Rehoboam's experience reminds me of an old story about Harry, a new man on the job, who was called to remove a large stump in a farmer's field. He didn't know how much dynamite to use, but pretended he did and hid behind his truck after he set the fuse. The dynamite exploded with a big boom! The stump went high in the air and landed on the cab of his truck. The old farmer said, "Young man, you only missed your goal by a few feet. A little more experience and you'll have those stumps landing in the truck bed every time." There wouldn't be any more time for Rehoboam to gain experience. His kingdom was divided within a few months. "When Israel saw that the king did not listen to them, the people answered the king saying, 'What portion do we have in David?'" (1 Kings 12:16, nasb).

They left and formed another nation at Shechem. His lack of wisdom brought him failure.

While there is wisdom to be gained from making mistakes, the best experience comes from learning how to gather the right information, develop the right communication skills, and build growing relationships with people who will follow your leadership. Wise leaders, whether in nations or churches, discover quickly that forcing people against their will to do something they do not want to do seldom brings favorable results. Rehoboam's decision is a case in point. In his whole life, up to this moment, he seldom had to compromise his actions with anyone. He developed the dangerous habit of getting his way at the expense of others who did not hold the power or position he held as Solomon's son. Lord Action's dictum "Power tends to corrupt, and absolute power corrupts absolutely" is applicable here (2004). Rehoboam believed that the king should always get his way. William Black says it poetically, "The strongest poison ever known came from Caesar's laurel crown" (Reader's Digest, 2005). Solomon came to the throne as David's heir at a difficult time. David had made many political enemies. Solomon learned from David's mistakes. Skillfully he consolidated his new kingdom by building a political and economic empire from new relationships he established with his neighbors.

Jared Diamond's book *Collapse* (2005) talks about nations and cultures that misused their experience and environment to gain the wisdom they needed to survive. His examples show how cultures destroyed themselves when they cut down all of the trees, overfished adjacent waters, or polluted their soils. He also shows how other societies in the same global latitude and similar circumstances learned by watching their neighbors fail. The result was a stewardship of the land and a successful posterity for their people. People are not always forgiving or tolerant when the attitude that we have always done it this way before or the king and his court always get the best and most while less powerful citizens get what is left over and unwanted. Dividing any organization, group or nation into those who make decisions and live in luxury and those who do the work and live in poverty is a plan time will soon destroy. Rehoboam must have missed those lessons and instead gathered his experience from his own generation in an environment of wealth and privilege. Rehoboam got what Dan Stanford said, "Experience is what you get when you don't get what you want" (1990). Nations spend billions on diplomacy to gain the wisdom that will give them a political or economic advantage to deal with another nation. David was known for his warrior instinct and military leadership. Solomon was known for his wisdom. But after their deaths, wisdom and leadership must have crossed over a generation because there does not seem to have been anything passed down to Rehoboam. Rehoboam's lack of wisdom and experience, coupled with his opulent environment, led him to make a disastrous decision. How, where, and when then does a person take from their environment the wisdom and experience needed to fashion the skills that can bring people together?

We experience the world first-hand via our senses. The objects and events of life, raw and uncut, enter our brains via our eyes and ears and other sensory avenues. What we see, hear, taste, and touch stimulates neural receptor cells that send electrochemical signals to the brain for processing. At first, raw information from the world around us momentarily rests at this early, sensory level. Called the "sensory store" or "sensory memory" by cognitive psychologists, this primary point of contact with the world allows us to see the world as it really is, without bias or "rose colored glasses," for just a moment (Sperling, 1960; Darwin, Turvey & Crowder, 1972). Once we start processing the information and associating it with knowledge and experiences already stored in memory, the information is changed. In the end, our understanding of the world around us may be close to the way it really is—accurate—or much different—inaccurate. Either way, this becomes our perception, or it governs our future thoughts and actions.

From our text, it is pretty clear that Rehoboam's ego, over-confidence, and information gathering skills were misguided. And yet, as William Glasser suggests, he believed his words with Jeroboam would be successful. What was lacking in Rehoboam's personality that led him to make such a destructive decision? He certainly believed he was making the right decision. People do believe that what they are doing will be successful or they wouldn't do it. Few leaders intentionally focus on failure. The feeling that our decisions are correct is part of a process known as "metacognition." Metacognition is thinking about thinking. It is knowing that we know what we know—or, at least, feeling that we know it. When you have something "on the tip of your tongue" you are experiencing a metacognitive phenomenon. Research suggests that our "feeling-of-knowing" something that we may not be able to recall is often quite accurate (Hart, 1965; Butterfield, Nelson & Peck, 1988). However, the feeling that we have made the right decision and actually being correct may be a completely different story. Other studies indicate that individuals often feel they are solving problems correctly when they are actually incorrect. They feel more confident in their solutions than those who solved the problem correctly (Metcalf, 1986; Metcalf and Jacobs [cited in Matlin, 1989]).

The logic of Rehoboam's plan for handling the northern tribes' request for kindness, in my mind, is certainly faulty. Why would he or any leader believe abusive words heaped on physical and economic hardship is the best way to build a productive relationship? I owe much of my success as a military officer to the fact that I spent the first three years coming up through the enlisted ranks from private to sergeant. I learned quickly that there are leaders who can get tasks done because they use their skills and knowledge about people in contrast with leaders who have to use their rank and authority to demand and cajole their people to get the same amount of work done. Wise leaders learn how to get workers to cooperate. The foolish leader uses words and actions that bring anger, resentment, and division in their workers. Our Lord's approach was to take some despised, rejected people in the community and turn them into willing disciples who would follow him anywhere. Rehoboam's method is similar to the approach in King Herod and Pilot's attitude in dealing with Jesus. They were in charge and made the situation fit their political agenda. History books seldom cover up leaders who practiced such foolish behaviors. Proverbs 4:19 says, "But the way of the wicked is like deep darkness; they do not know what makes them stumble" (nasb). When a person's attitude lacks kindness and compassion, they create a host of problems for themselves and others. While the abuser continues to fall over their own egocentric foolishness and behavior, the abused will continue to suffer from a lack of kindness and compassion.

The way to avoid such failure is to begin with your perception about people. Do you believe that your education, wealth, or some other factor makes you better or superior to them? Does your attitude about their present condition take away and/or destroy their dignity and self-esteem? If these thoughts and behaviors are true about you, then your perception about people will cloud and influence decisions you may make toward building more positive relationships. Perceptions can be changed with understanding and information gained by digging deeper for the facts about your own psyche. Why do you need to feel and say the things you say? Do you have low self-esteem? Are you afraid that if you treat others with kindness and compassion they will take advantage of you? Maybe it is time to look inward at yourself if you are having problems building relationships. What events in your past have shaped your ability to build lasting fruitful relationships? When you look in the mirror, the face you see is the person you must begin with to build better relationships.

Here is a process that might work for you if your present responses are not working as well as you desire. Change may be your best option but it also may be the most difficult one to make. Ask yourself what other possible solutions and choices might you make instead of the one you considered. For example, you expressed your anger and disappointment because the person you were working with did not fully carry out your instructions as you directed. Ask yourself, *Were my instructions written out? Did I assume too much? Did the person lack the motor skills and/or training necessary to complete this task in the manner I desired?* Remember, "Everything that irritates us about others can lead us to an understanding of ourselves" (Jung, 2006). If the answer to any of these questions is yes, then the problem may be with you and not the other person. Many times faulty perceptions and assumptions lead to conclusions that are the opposite of what is intended (Binns, 2007).

Good communication is another leader's key to success. We see this in churches, business, and government when there is a change in leadership. Those who cannot communicate their goals and ideals doom those who follow them to failure or mediocrity. Some leaders have a natural talent for communication. Others learned by experience and from the school of hard knocks. The book of Proverbs gives us wisdom and truths that are useful to those who lead or follow. A wise person is careful about what he/she says and considers the consequences their words will bring. The fool speaks without thinking and discovers too late that his/her words have destroyed a relationship. Solomon's proverbs provide us with examples about the wise and the foolish. Reading them often will imprint them on your mind and heart for use in difficult situations.

Using the Golden Rule is a great way to begin decision-making. Our text situation began with words of wisdom from the elders to Rehoboam, "If you treat them with kindness…they will follow you" (1 Kings 12:7, nasb). And it ended with division, anger, and hatred. When Israel saw that the king did not listen to them, the people answered the king saying, 'What portion do we have in David?'" (1 Kings 12:16, nasb). Is that what you would have wanted? Too bad Rehoboam didn't heed his elders' kind words instead of choosing to respond with the wrong words from his friends. He might have saved his nation. Great solutions begin with the right words. Great leaders say the right words and follow through with the right actions. This elicits others to follow their leadership. Sometimes it is not the best road to go with your friends.

For Further Bible Study

1. In David's reign there were men who spoke maliciously against him and it cost them their lives. Who were those David named, asking Solomon to close out their accounts?

2. Contrast the speech made by one of David's enemies in question 1 above with the words written about Solomon in 1 Kings 4:29–34 (nasb). What, in your estimation, did Solomon have that those who spoke about against David didn't have?

3. Was Rehoboam's only mistake his words spoken to Jeroboam?

For Personal Growth

1. Can you remember a time when your ego and/or self-esteem got in the way of your success? What brought you back to an acceptable form of behavior? How could you share this information with family or friends?

2. Dr. Cupp wrote in this chapter, "Once we start processing the information and associating it with knowledge and experiences already stored in memory, the information is changed. In the end, our understanding of the world around us may be close to the way it really is (accurate) or much different (inaccurate). Either way, this becomes our perception, or it governs our future thoughts and actions."

   Next time you are confronted with a need to make a decision about something, write down your perceptions and how you understand the problem or situation. Then ask yourself if your perceptions are correct or do you need more information to make the right decision

3. If you are not making good decisions, your local public library is a good source where can you go for information on how to make better decisions.

THE SERVANT SAID TO NAAMAN...

"IF HE ASKED YOU TO DO SOME GREAT THING..."

2 KINGS 5:10–14

THE RIGHT WORDS CAREFULLY CHOSEN MAKE A DIFFERENCE.

Life is difficult and sometimes emotionally complicated. When you are on the bottom of the social ladder,
people tend to look down on you and reject everything
about you from your lifestyle to who you are as a person. Years ago I was privileged to know a family named
Pope. They had seven children. The youngest then was
a little five-year-old guy named Benjamin. I asked him
one day how he was doing. Benjamin smiled up at me
and said, "Life is hard when you are the littlest Pope."
Yes! Life can be hard, even if you are named Pope, but

doubly difficult when you are the youngest in a large family of brothers and sisters.

Naaman didn't have a name or a family problem. As the Syrian army commander, he had already climbed the mountains of political and social acceptance. Only the king was greater and held more power. Naaman was comfortable with an army of thousands obeying his commands and orders. His word meant life or death for those conquered by his army. Scripture tells us he was highly regarded as a valiant solider by the Syrian king…but all of this was about to change for he had one glaring problem. Naaman was a leper. Leprosy, in Naaman's day, was an incurable disease, causing the sufferer to become ostracized much the same way as some diseases and illnesses do today. I sometimes believe that those at the top of the political and social ladder have a harder time adjusting to their own personal illness and disease than those who are at the bottom. Why? Could it be that those at the top are used to a life going well, getting their way, and surviving where the poor more often fail. Certainly they have more resources to buy better food and provide quality health care. Naaman was definitely in that group. Despite his social standing and victories over his enemies, leprosy was a condition he could not conquer. Then one day a young girl, an Israeli captive who served Naaman's wife, said to her mistress, "I wish that my master were with the prophet who is in Samaria! Then he would cure him of his leprosy" (2 Kings 5:3, nasb). When those words came to

Naaman, he probably responded like many would today thinking, *"Well I have tried everything else and found nothing works, I might as well try the prophet of God in Israel."* Of course the Lord who created us can heal us. And no, there is nothing wrong with asking God for healing. Putting our faith in the Lord opens the door to the power of God's healing. Sooner is always better than later.

Naaman went to his king telling him about the healing powers of the prophet in Israel. The king liked the idea and sent a letter to the king of Israel recommending Naaman for treatment. Because leprosy was incurable, the king's request frightened Israel's king into believing it was a trap to pick a quarrel with him. He tore his clothing as a sign of humility. When word about the letter reached the prophet Elisha he asked that Naaman be sent to him at his house. Naaman arrived; very excited thinking that Elisha would come out and call on his God wave his hand over the place and cure his leprosy. But he had no such luck. A messenger came from Elisha's house and told Naaman, "Go, wash yourself seven times in the Jordan [River] and your flesh will be restored" (2 Kings 5:10, nasb). How dare this prophet send a servant instead of coming himself! Naaman's anger was kindled by the servant's words, and in a rage he turned to leave.

Anger and rage are initially tied to our "fight or flight reflex." This survival mechanism is designed to prepare us to escape or meet potentially threatening situations. The strong emotions of fear, anger, or rage place us in a state of physiological arousal. Our respiration increases, our heart starts pumping faster, and our pupils dilate in order to let in more light. We are ready to run or retaliate! In one sense, this makes us sharper and more attuned to the stimuli around us, but strong emotion can have its downside. Studies on "mood congruence" suggest that we recall information better when the mood during recall is the same as the mood during the time we first learned the information (Bower, 1992; Schacter, 1999). But being in a state of anger, anxiety, or depression can actually reduce our performance over time and interfere with our ability to process information (Darke, 1988). With strong emotional states, we are open to distractions and clouded thinking (Ellis & Ashbrook, 1988).

While anger can be a survival instinct that helps us to overcome a deadly or fearful situation, it isn't a long-term behavior that is beneficial for the mind, body, or those with whom you live and work. Yes, anger is one option and a possible solution to a problem, but too often it is chosen without regard to other options that bring less stress on the body or one that can build relationships instead of tearing them down. An angry Naaman was about to leave and head for home saying, "Are not the waters of the Abana and Pharpar in Damascus better than the waters of Israel?" (2 Kings 5:12, nasb). Whether these waters were better or not was not the issue here. The issue before Naaman was really simple. Did he want to be cleansed of his leprosy? His anger had removed his logic and purpose for coming. His assumption was that the prophet would come out to see him. Instead, the prophet sent his servant with a message about washing in the Jordan River. Now Naaman had become like the "littlest Pope." He was no longer in charge. His power and authority were taken away, and he was asked to do something he did not want to do. For one who was used to associating with the rich and famous, he now was listening to a servant give him instructions. This was an insult to his position as the Syrian army commander. He viewed this message as an attack on his ego. One might guess that Naaman's thinking was, *Better to be a leper in Syria than wash in Israel's dirty Jordan River.* One of Naaman's servants, wanting the best for his master, tried to reason with him, saying, "Master, if the prophet had asked you to do some great thing, would you have not done it? The servant's logic was perfect saying, 'How much more then when he asks you to do this simple thing…wash and be healed'" (2 Kings 5:13, nasb). The servant's encouragement worked, and Naaman's logic and reason returned. Then Naaman washed in the Jordan River as Elisha directed and his flesh was restored as perfect as the skin on a new baby. The servant's simple words gave Naaman the encouragement he needed to complete his mission.

This is a wonderful story with a happy ending. However, it almost ended in tragedy because Naaman was foolishly going to let his pride and anger destroy the very thing he came for and wanted most. What I find in this story that is more interesting than his anger is that it is his own servants that convinced him to wash in the waters in Israel. Those same servants, who normally were powerless to create change or influence their master, said the right words to save the day and heal his disease. Pride and anger are often tied together as a viable combination for dealing with people and problems. Sometimes pride and anger quickly elevate the problem to where there is no rational solution. When used inappropriately pride and anger add stress and frustration to problem solving. Solomon said, "Better is the end of a thing than the beginning thereof: and the patient in spirit is better than the proud in spirit" (Ecclesiastes 7:8, kjv). This battle was won by a servant's logic and well-chosen words.

Naaman's career as the Syrian army commander may have been the cause for his irrational behavior. In battle he was probably a creative and logical battlefield tactician. He carefully plotted battle phases and strategies needed for victory. He had control over his own emotions and those in his forces. His men looked up to him and trusted his leadership. His experience and battle record proved his skill and abilities. But none of these factors and characteristics were present when he came to Israel. He fell into the trap that catches many leaders. Experience works best when it can be repeated in the same place, under the same or equal conditions and involving the same or similar people. Naaman was out of his element. He was in Samaria, not Syria. He was not at war, but at peace. He was not the one in charge, but a sick man in need of someone's help for healing. His experience on the battlefield and his command over soldiers in Syria was useless when he stood before Elisha's home in Israel. When his pride was hurt and his authority questioned, he entered into unfamiliar territory and a new experience. He tried to solve his new situation by expressing his anger and frustration with Elisha's servant, and it wasn't working. Seldom will commanders admit weakness, loss of cognition, or an unclear understanding of the battlefield situation. Why? It is too easy to get angry and blame someone else as reason for the problem.

Let's put this story into a modern setting. You purchased a new home appliance at a store in another town yesterday, and today it doesn't work. You take the time to find all the papers, packing materials, and your store receipt. Then you repack the appliance and drive back to the store where you purchased it and ask the clerk at the counter for a refund or a replacement. The person who sold it to you isn't working today. The new sales person you are speaking to is not experienced and does not have the authority to make the decision to exchange or refund your money. She asks you to return later or wait until the supervisor, who is in a meeting, can help you. You have done everything you know to do. Now patience and kindness are running thin. Your anger begins to kindle, and your voice gets louder. You feel that you are not getting the respect and treatment due a customer. You are not a crook, nor someone trying to take advantage of the store or its merchandise. This store must have incompetent leadership because they have stupid rules. You start to get angry because there is nothing more you can do except come back again. So what's the real problem here? Like most people in a similar situation, you feel somewhat justified in using anger. So when your pride is injured you feel okay to accept anger as a solution where you would normally reject it, thinking, *I don't normally act this way, but now you are forcing me to get angry.* Is anger the only solution, or are there other solutions that you could consider first? One problem with experience is that it usually works best when repeated in the same situations over and over again. But even then there is no assurance your past experience will work every time. The danger of using a past experience in a different situation is that there is no guarantee that it will work in a new or different circumstance. Little Benjamin Pope found out that when he gained some new experience it would not always work in every situation. Naaman's frustration with Elisha aggravated his desire to find the solution he wanted for his leprosy. The problem was simply that Elisha's proposed solution did not fit with Naaman's assumption and experience.

Many faith groups are confronted with this same problem when they find their morals and values are in conflict with current cultural changes going on in their community. They expect the present situation to conform to their past experiences as Naaman did. However, yesterday's values and rules will not always agree with today's cultural needs and wants. One simple example is the place African Americans and women now have and hold in society today. Race and gender now have equal standing before the law. Blacks are no longer willing to take a seat at the back of the bus nor are women content with a policy that says they cannot have equal opportunity in employment. As culture changes yesterday's answers and solutions often come into conflict with today's lifestyles. Sometimes we believe if yesterday's answers are trumpeted loud enough with lots of enthusiasm and emotion, society will agree with us. Theology cannot be separated from culture, and culture is changing more rapidly than at any time in our nation's history. The end result is strife; anger and frustration when events like Naaman's do not go our way. Naaman's name was respected in Syria. Why shouldn't he have that same respect in front of Elisha's house? When it didn't happen, he thought, *When Elisha's servants see my anger, they will go and tell him and then he will come out and call on the name of his God to heal me.* You can be assured that when Naaman got angry on a battlefield his soldiers or servants moved out quickly and smartly to see that things were done the way the commander wanted them done or they would receive the consequence for disobedience. Isn't my way always the right way?

May I share an example of a cultural-theological battle going on in our churches today? American Protestant church music during the forties, fifties, and sixties generally held to the traditional songs in the hymnbook. Choir anthems, solos, trios, and quartets were always acceptable. Then a major change began to take place. Gospel songs and choruses entered the worship experience in the seventies and eighties. Some church leaders, to the consternation of their membership, added electronic keyboards, guitars, drums, and band instruments to their worship. Many church leaders and elderly members resented these changes taking place in their church. Traditional music was phased out, as younger members wanted more and more up-tempo music with a beat for congregational music and worship. Those who decided these changes were good saw a host of young adults won to the Lord through music and returned to church. But this gain was not made without a cost. Many senior adults and others left churches with blended or contemporary music programs and searched until they found churches where the music was still biblical and/or traditional. In these cases, where doctrine and polity clashed with culture, culture won as some church members were forced to consider moving to another church. My theory is that both old and young adults were trying to hold on to their music experience even if they had to move or create a different church's worship to get it. Their perception is, *what is right for us is good for everyone, even if it rips the church apart by taking church worship in two different directions.* Those who wouldn't change went looking for a place where the past could be repeated to match their experience. Those who wanted change moved or changed things until they got what they wanted and it met their needs regardless of who got hurt. While such a statement may be harsh, my experience is that it happened all too often.

Fortunately for Naaman, his servant was able to view his problem from a different perspective. They helped Naaman set aside his ego and experience for the right solution to his problem. Naaman's servant saw it as one of obedience to Elisha's message, to wash in the Jordan River seven times and become clean. It was not an issue of who held the power, but simple instructions for a desired solution. The only person Naaman ever had to be obedient to was his king back in Syria. Naaman's experience had led him to believe life might be complicated and sometimes issues were complex, but time and again his experience had proven to him that his solutions were the right ones. Now his problem was that his solution would not give him the goal he so desperately wanted. He made the problem more complicated by inserting his ego into the situation. Naaman assumed that since his leprosy required special treatment, Elisha should come out and call upon his God or wave his hand over the leprosy spot and heal him. Life may be complex at times, but sometimes a best solution is to follow the instructions carefully and obediently to get to the desired results.

A servant's simple request to be obedient to Elisha's instruction may sound too simplistic for today's cell phone, digital, gadget-filled world. Sometimes when looking for answers and solutions to life's problems, it is helpful to stand outside the problem and look at it from a different perspective. Pretend you are someone else looking at your problem. How would your mom, dad, or a good friend solve your problem? Faith and obedience may seem like tools too simple for the modern world. But they are some of the best tools and resources to get the right solution. "If only my master would go and see the prophet in Israel," said the little maid to Naaman's wife. What does a child know about leprosy? If the physicians can't heal the patient, how would a child's words help in this situation? The young maid remembered the prophet's miracles, which led her to speak out. She only asked Naaman to go to the prophet's house. His leprosy and need for healing led him to consider her words. And it was his servants who asked him to change and try the waters of the Jordan and find wellness that brought the healing he desired. Neither did they have anything they needed to prove. Their motives were pure. Maybe the servants had more faith than Naaman. I believe there is no end to what you can do for others if you are motivated by the Lord to speak without adding your advice and ego into the situation.

Words carefully chosen and rightly spoken make the difference between success and failure. If his servants had remained silent, Naaman would have died from his disease, separated from those he loved and no longer in favor with his king. After washing in the Jordan seven times and finding his skin as new as a baby's, he headed for home restored and rejoicing. A few simple words from servants and Naaman's obedience made the difference. Remember this the next time someone is overcome with a problem they can't solve and shares it with you. Help them exercise their faith and obedience, and let God do the rest. I wish I'd said that. Don't you?

For Further Bible Study

1. With all we know and understand about anger it is still a problem for many people. What wisdom does Solomon give us in Proverbs 15:16 (nasb)?

2. Second Kings 5 follows the story of Naaman with one about Gehazi. Contrast these two men and list their similarities and differences. What can you learn from their behaviors?

3. In what way did Nathan successfully handle David's

anger to bring about his repentance in 2 Samuel 12 (nasb)?

For Personal Growth

1. Pick one or two stories out of your local newspaper where someone's anger and/or selfishness brought about disastrous results. Then analyze how the problem could have been solved or avoided without anger? Would your methodology work for most people in a similar situation?

2. Who is someone you know who seldom uses anger as a methodology to get what they want accomplished? Have you ever told them that you appreciate this characteristic in their lifestyle?

3. What special characteristics do you think the servants possessed that allowed them to bring wisdom to Naaman? Is this a characteristic you would like to have? How might you go about developing it?

THE LEPERS SAID TO THE GATEKEEPERS...

"THERE IS NO ONE THERE."

2 KINGS 7:10

COMPASSION COMES FROM A LOVING HEART.

What determines if news is good or bad? Bad news sells newspapers, makes the television evening news, and stirs people to action. Good news may or may not do any of these. Bad news may be good for those who sell news, but bad for those who read or hear it. If it is good news for you, does that mean it is good news for everyone else? Maybe not! What are the best words to use when sharing good or bad news? Is our silence better than telling the bad news? And then there is the question: when is the right time to make good or bad news public? Each of us will, of course, answer these questions a little differently. Some of us want to know more about what the news is before we decide to tell it. Others may be too quick to tell it before they check their sources. Then they have to figure out how to handle this added problem if their source for the news is false. I no longer have the source for this old story, but it does show how difficult it is to respond to good or bad news.

"How is your wife?" a man asked his friend he hadn't seen for years.

"She's in heaven," his friend replied.

"Oh, I'm sorry," said the man. Then he realized that this was not a good thing to say, so he added, "I mean, I'm glad." And that sounded even worse, so finally came up with "Well, I'm surprised." Most of us have had such an experience when, with the best intentions, what we said about the news sounded worse than saying nothing at all.

Our text tells us that when Syria's King Benhadad besieged the city of Samaria there were four lepers living outside the city wall. With the Syrian army in front of them, the wall and the city behind them, they reasoned, "Why do we sit here until we die? If we say, enter the city, the famine is in the city and we will die there, and if we stay here we shall die also. Therefore, let us go over to the camp of the Syrians. If they spare us we shall live; if they kill us we shall but die" (2 Kings 7:4, nasb). Covered with leprosy and starving from the siege, they reasoned that they were going to die anyway, so if the Syrians fed them, at least they would live a little longer. When they arrived at the camp they discovered that the Syrians had fled, leaving everything behind. Starving, they quickly filled their stomachs with food. After feasting on Syrian food, the lepers began to think about the situation back in the city and decided that something needed to be done. One leper, in a compassionate moment, said, "What we are doing is not right. This day is a day of good news, but we are keeping silent" (2 Kings 7:4, nasb). At least one of the lepers began to feel guilty for not sharing their discovery. He felt they needed to tell the starving folks back in the city what was available to them outside the city walls.

We all know there are times to speak and times to remain silent. The trick is to know when to tell what you know and when to wait for a better opportunity or just remain silent. And yet sometimes silence is cowardly and unfair to those who need the information we have. William Henry once said in a *Chicago Tribune* article, "Fools live to regret their words, wise men to regret their silence." Deciding they could no longer remain silent, the four lepers trekked back to the city to share their discovery. The lepers felt guilty for remaining silent after feasting on the Syrian food when those who had been besieged in the city were starving. This event still had many unanswered questions, which might determine whether this was good news or not. Would the Syrians return? Why had the Syrians left all this food behind? Was the food poisoned? The lepers were in a difficult situation. Should they tell what they knew and let others decide for themselves what was still unknown? Or should they keep silent until they had more information? Food had been their main goal and objective. Then finding the camp empty and food available, they determined they should share the good news.

Thousands of times each year the Apostle Peter's actions are judged as cowardly when he stood before the fire in Caiaphas's courtyard and said, "I do not know the man" (Matthew 26:72, nasb). Now contrast that event with the one in the book of Acts where Peter and John are brought before the council to defend their actions for healing the man at the temple gate. Peter speaking of Jesus' resurrection and power to heal said, "We can not stop speaking what we have seen and heard" (Acts 4:20, nasb). Peter is the major character in both events. Jesus was the reason for his silence in Caiaphas's courtyard and the reason for the boldness before the council. Was Jesus the good news or not? Almost all good news does need to be told, but when? And some silence is golden, but for how long? Like Peter we discover it is not always an easy choice. What may be one person's wisdom to keep silent is viewed by another person as cowardice. The lepers went back to the city and told the gatekeepers, who then told the king that the Syrian camp was empty and there was food and spoils for the taking. It was good news; the city would no longer starve. The lepers wanted them to open the gates and come out and enjoy the food the Lord had provided. The king, safe in the city, did not intend to die today in the Syrian camp. His response to the lepers' message was "This is not good news, but a Syrian trick." He said the Syrians have "hid themselves in a field waiting for us to come out of the city, to capture us and get into the city" (2 Kings 7:12–13, nasb). The king did not receive the lepers' words as good news. He has a role as king to maintain and a city to protect. He was not ready to leave a place he knew was secure for the possible treachery that lay in the Syrian camp. While neither the king nor the lepers were positive they have all the facts, both were sure they had the right words that would lead the city to take the right action. The king's interpretation was totally opposite from the lepers'. The good news was now bad news. As is often the case, even in our own day, two people can interpret almost any event differently. When this happens those involved come to an impasse. [Note: I've corrected some of the verb tenses of the lepers' story here so they are consistently in past tense.]

The next verse in this text is classic. It offers a pragmatic approach to the lepers and king's impasse. A servant listening to the discussion thought, *What have we got to lose? Let's send someone out and see if this is true.* He used the same logic as the lepers used, that they are going to die anyway if they stayed inside the walls, but added a new idea: let's protect the city and send someone out to see what is going on! The servant took what information and interpretations were available and determined a safe way to come to a rational decision. The servant's approach broke the stalemate. Sometimes just considering more than one person's thinking about a problem can lead to a better solution.

Words used to trap and fool people are an ancient methodology that catches the gullible as well as the wise. However, once fooled the wise are harder to convince the next time. It could be said that wisdom is the skillful use of knowledge gained through experience. It could also be said that wisdom is the ability to not make the same mistake twice. The process used by the human brain to develop this kind of wisdom is linked to the brain's ability to acquire skills and expertise. Expertise is more than just knowing...it's intentionally doing the right things. Cognitive theorists have tried to explain the process. Fitts and Posner (1967) postulated that we begin in a *cognitive stage,* memorizing the correct set of rules or steps for any concept or procedure. We apply or practice the rules or steps in real life and make preliminary mistakes. This is followed by an *associative stage,* where we internally review and eliminate mistakes. After time (sometimes years) the task becomes second nature, and we enter the *autonomous stage.* Interestingly, there is evidence that what we call wisdom may not be a higher brain function. Fairly recent neuropsychological research suggests that the higher functioning prefrontal cortex may be involved only at the beginning, when we learn something new and try to analyze or organize it. Later, as the knowledge becomes automatic (wisdom), the part of the brain most active is the more primitive mid-brain where memory processes are located (Jenkins, et al., 1994).

Truth in communication is essential to the success of any individual or society. Our whole basis for interaction with people is based on believing what people tell us is the truth. In our culture words are always true unless we know or can prove otherwise. Think what life would be like if you didn't believe what anyone said. All human communication would come to a standstill. We couldn't help anyone because we would not be sure what we wanted to do was based on truth or falsehood and whether our actions would be good or bad. Our minds would have difficulty categorizing truth. For more than twenty years Brazilian show promoters, gossip columnists, and political figures kept assuring the people of Brazil that singer Frank Sinatra was coming to Brazil. He had never promised he would. And so it became a national joke. People would say, "Sure you will marry me when Frank Sinatra comes to Brazil." Then one day Sinatra announced he was going to sing in Rio at the 200,000-seat soccer stadium. It was on the front page of every newspaper with huge headlines. Almost every story carried the line, "…this time it is true." I am sure that there were a few people who even up to the time Sinatra arrived and sang at the stadium thought that it really was another hoax. Israel's king might as well have lived in Brazil and in modern times because until the news came back that the camp was empty and the Syrians were not waiting, he was a skeptic (*Prairie Overcomer* magazine). Was the leper's decision to share their information more altruistic than the king's interpretation to keep the city safe by staying inside the walls? Both had put the information before them on a hierarchy of value and sought to make an altruistic and compassionate decision.

Altruism is "the disposition to act in behalf of others for unselfish reasons" (Chaplin, 1985). It is as much externally determined (social) as it is internal (cognitive). Research suggests that a crowd can have an effect on our altruistic behavior, no matter what our internal beliefs. In fact, studies indicate that the more bystanders there are to an incident of victimization, the less likely will be the chance that anyone will help (Clarkson, 1996; Latane & Rodin, 1969). Remember the example of Peter before the fire. Only he knew the real reason for his denial and silence. But our unselfish acts are undeniably tied to who we are, and to how strong our feelings of risk, responsibility, and empathy are. Bias also plays a role. We tend, sadly, to help only those who are like us (Krebs, 1975).

Our minds are continually bombarded with new information from the media, family, friends, neighbors, ministers, and politicians. How do we know when someone speaks the truth? Almost daily we read or hear that someone said or printed something that was supposed to be true when they knew it wasn't. It is a sad commentary on the media and our national leaders when words are used so often to intentionally mislead or deceive us rather than tell us the truth. Sometimes we are a little too gullible. On other occasions we are deliberately deceived or exploited for someone else's gain. Watergate, Irangate, Travelgate, and many other gates yet to be named, are just a few examples how the general public is manipulated. Dick Armey spoke about trust just before a presidential election. Quoted in *Reader's Digest,* he said that there are, "Three groups of people (who) spend other people's money: children, thieves, and politicians. All three (will) need supervision" (2000). Would I be far from the truth in saying there may be even a few theologians, pastors, and church folks who have their own agenda for telling half-truths and even untruths so they can stay in power, increase their income or influence? It is not unheard of for clergy to alter a university transcript to give them a degree they did not earn. Some human resource directors have indicated that most résumés contain at least one falsehood. For some hopeful employees, it is easier for them to tell the lie than to tell the truth. "It is said that power corrupts, but actually it's more true that power attracts the corruptible" (Brin, 2007).

Israel's king didn't believe that the good news was true. He was sure it was a trick set up by the Syrians. Before we think, *how sad,* remember most of us have fallen into a similar trap that was set for us. Some of us have fallen into the trap more times than we want to admit to or remember. If you have compassion for people in need, I guarantee you have been told sad stories that are partly or totally untrue. However, just because half-truths and lies are propagated on the public every day doesn't mean we must accept them or participate in them. It is true that with the poor and needy sometimes the situation seems to demand it. However wisdom and discernment are skills readily needed when working with people in need.

The Bible tells us kings had priests and prophets to help with understanding what truth was. But when things got tough, sometimes even the king didn't believe God's message or messenger was true. In our text this event was brought on because the Lord had told Elisha to say to the king, "Tomorrow about this time a measure of fine flour shall be sold for a shekel and two measures of barley for a shekel in the gate of Samaria" (2 Kings 7:18, n a s b). The famine together with the siege by Syria was devastating the city. Chapter 6 tells us they were even practicing cannibalism. The situation was so bad that they couldn't accept the promise the Lord gave through the prophet was true. I love this quote from *Our Daily Bread: "A* strong faith sees the invisible, believes the incredible, and receives the impossible" (1992). Faith, like many of the citizens in the city, was dying.

Think about this with me for a moment. An airplane operates on two physical laws or principles. The first is the law of gravity and the second law of aerodynamics. If it is ever to fly, it must choose one over the other. It cannot do both at the same time. When at 145 knots a supersonic aircraft pilot pulls back on the stick, the law of gravity loses. As long as the pilot maintains enough air speed, the heavier-than-air craft will remain in flight. The moment the air speed is lessened, gravity will take over again, and the aircraft will start descending. When we choose to believe that God is able, we leave the world of the impossible and live in the world of the possible. Like the pilot we must pull back on the stick of our own will and take the trip on faith that we can overcome the impossible (1975). In the king's unbelieving nightmare, a hungry servant makes a suggestion that if they didn't go out they are going to die of hunger. If this was a trick and they died out there, it would only be like the "…the men of Israel who have already perished, so let's send someone out to see. The king sent two chariots with men saying, 'Go and see'" (2 Kings 7:13–14, nasb). Good news is only good news when you are committed to it. Sadly today many are like the king, raised in a religious tradition but never considering how to tie their commitment to their faith in God. Rick Warren in 2002 wrote *The Purpose Driven Life,* saying, "For many people the barrier to spiritual growth is not lack of commitment, but over-commitment to the wrong things." One needs not to look far to see how many of us are overly committed to material things resulting in a weak faith that God will and can provide for us. The king, and possibly others, felt they were safer starving inside the walls than taking the risk and going out to the Syrian camp and satisfying their hunger. Christians need to remember that there are risks we should consider, for good reasons, as an exercise to our faith commitment.

When do we perceive the need for change? What words lead us to change our overt actions or covert thoughts? Psychologically speaking, there is not one answer to these questions. There are many theories. Drive theorists, like Hull, believed that we change when we sense an imbalance in our system and wish to restore the balance so that a state of "homeostasis" exists (Hull, 1943). Perhaps this could explain why change often follows a period of discomfort or confusion. When things start to contradict in our minds, when beliefs or solutions no longer work for us, when the world stops making sense, and when we feel an inner imbalance, we immediately seek to make changes. Some psychologists call this "cognitive dissonance"—an inner struggle between contradictory thoughts, which, if unchanged, can lead to psychological turmoil (Festinger, 1957).

How and when do you know your faith is the foundation for your life and not just something to use in an emergency? Back in my 101st Airborne Division days I remember the first time I saw a real parachute jump. I sat in the bleachers at one side of the drop zone. Thirteen troop carrier airplanes flew overhead and paratroopers began exiting the doors on both sides of the aircraft. I watched as hundreds safely floated down to the ground. I believed that day I could do what they were doing. It looked so easy to put on a parachute and make a safe parachute jump. But when did I really believe? About three weeks later when I found myself standing in the door of an Air Force C-123 aircraft and the jumpmaster said, "You're next, stand in the door…go." I left a good safe aircraft and trusted my parachute to take me safely down to the ground. Faith is like that. You have to trust it and put your weight on it and then it will work for you.

It was the king's servant who solved the problem first and correctly. He reasoned, *The best thing we can do is to go out and see if the Syrians are waiting to trap us and we will die. But if they have fled and the good news is true then we will live…send someone out to find out if what we heard is true.* He was willing to put his weight (right actions) on the fact that the good news (right words) was true. The lepers didn't make their decision until their stomachs were full. The king wouldn't make his decision until the chariots returned with the news that the Syrians had fled. If you had been one of these three, how would you have responded to the good news?

Like the *Survivor* television show, reality sometimes is quite different from how we imagine it. It is one thing to believe people can eat bugs and snakes in a soup. Reality sets in when the soup is in the bowl in front of you. The lepers didn't fully accept the reality of the moment in the Syrian camp until their stomachs started to get full. Then they realized their error and hurried back to the city to tell the good news. One leper said, "What we are doing is not right" (2 Kings

7:9, NASB). FILLED WITH COMPASSION FOR THEIR FRIENDS BACK IN THE CITY, THEY HURRIED BACK WITH A STORY TO TELL GOOD NEWS IS WORTH SHARING EVEN IF SOME ARE NOT READY TO BELIEVE IT. LET'S GO NOW AND SHARE THIS GOOD NEWS WITH THOSE WHO ARE HUNGRY, BEFORE WHAT WE HAVE TAKES AWAY OUR EXCITEMENT TO HELP OTHERS.

For Further Bible Study

1. Who was the woman who felt compassion for Moses when he was a baby in a basket? Do you think it was easier for her to have compassion for him than for the lepers to have compassion on the city? (Exodus 2) Why?

2. Pharaoh had a dream he could not interpret (Genesis 41). Name the person who had to tell Pharaoh the good and bad news about his dream. Did this person soft-soap the information or lay the truth out before him?

3. Can you find the miracle where God called a warrior to reduce the size of his army and then use strange weapons to defeat the Midianites and Amalekites? (Judges 7) Did this warrior believe the message was true when it was given to him? Was the test he devised an act of faith or doubt?

For Personal Growth

1. Take a sheet of paper and write a paragraph about how you feel when a homeless or street person asks you for money to buy food. Try to identify your mixed feelings like: help versus frustration, fear versus love, and kindness versus apathy.

2. Would you have compassion on a homeless person and give them money to buy food? How would you know if he used the money for food or to support a drug or alcohol addiction? What alternatives might be available if you looked into other ways to meet his needs?

3. Use the Internet to look up "homeless solutions." Select one or two articles and look for new information on this difficult subject.

Words of
Power and
Action

ELISHA SAID TO ELIJAH...

"PLEASE LET A DOUBLE PORTION OF
YOUR SPIRIT COME BE UPON ME."

2 KINGS 2:9

SOMETIMES IT IS NOT WHAT YOU ASK FOR, BUT WHAT YOU INTEND TO DO WITH IT THAT DETERMINES IF YOU'LL GET IT.

Being the best you can be has always been a worthy goal whether you are a president, prime minister, politician, or preacher. Usually great leaders are pleased when their achievements and successes are recorded for posterity and their mistakes overlooked. Even before American presidents retire from office, planning starts for a library to hold their memoirs. Presidents Eisenhower, Nixon, Carter, Reagan, Bush, and Clinton all have built libraries to hold their historical material. While many books may be written about a president when they are living, how a nation really evaluates their work starts after their death. Greatness is always viewed differently depending upon who is making the determination and when they are making it. Winston Churchill, for example, served as Lord of the Admiralty in 1911 and became the scapegoat for England's military failure in the Gallipoli campaign against the Turks. Then he was elected Prime Minister after Neville Chamberlain's appeasement with Hitler failed and Germany invaded the Netherlands, Belgium, and France. Then, after his brilliant successes during World War II, his government was turned out when England's populace rejected him a second time. It is sad that many great leaders have to die before they receive their nation's thanks for a job well done. Maybe the real histories can only be written after you retire from office or die. You may have watched the public funeral services for Presidents Ronald Reagan and Gerald Ford. At both funerals there were those who grieved and those who demonstrated. But, for the most part, the kudos and kind words overshadowed the complaints. It was interesting to me that television commentators said so many good things about both these former presidents, which was just the opposite from media opinions about them during their presidencies. During their presidencies the media bombarded the public with statements about their character, abilities, and shortcomings. If my perception is correct, it seems that the correct methodology is to criticize their work while they are living and laud their greatness after they are gone.

Elijah, like Churchill, Reagan, and Ford, was not a popular leader with kings and other leaders in his day. He challenged the prophets of Baal on Mt. Carmel and won a stunning victory as the Lord answered his call with fire and took up the sacrificial oxen, the altar, and the water in the trench. His encounters with Ahab and Jezebel were hardly cordial. After his success at Mt. Carmel, Jezebel's wrath sent him fleeing for his life to Mt. Horeb. Elijah's prominence with the people returned after Syria was defeated. But, he never won Ahab's approval nor with Ahab's successors, Ahaziah and Jehoram. We all know that you will not win all of life's battles, but it is nice to be remembered that you did win a few that counted. Second Kings 2 tells us about the end of Elijah's ministry to Israel. The Lord set up an itinerary for Elijah's last few days. On each occasion as Elijah announced his next destination to Elisha, his disciple, and said, "You stay here." But Elisha replied, "As the Lord lives and you yourself live, I will not leave you" (2 Kings 2:2, nasb). So they traveled together until Elijah came to Jericho and then moved on to the Jordan River where again Elijah requested Elisha remain. And again Elisha refused. The two crossed over the Jordan River on dry ground and on the other side Elijah said, "Ask what I shall do for you before I am taken from you." And Elisha said, "Please, let a double portion of your spirit come upon me" (2 Kings 2:9, nasb). Elijah suggested such a request was very difficult and put a condition on the request that if Elisha saw him taken up into heaven his request would be granted. Horses and chariots of fire separated the two, and Elijah was taken up in a whirlwind to heaven. Elisha saw all this, tore his clothes, and picked up the mantle that had fallen from Elijah as he was taken up. Elisha, with Elijah's mantle and a double portion of his spirit, then divided the waters of the Jordan and returned to the place where they stood before crossing over. When the sons of the prophets saw him coming they said, "The spirit of Elijah rests on Elisha" (2 Kings 2:15, nasb). He had received what he asked for. Now what would the Lord have in store for him in the work of the kingdom?

If you or I were in a similar position as these two, master and disciple, would you ask for a single or double portion of your master's spirit? If I could read your mind and thoughts they might go something like this: *Well that depends. If I have to confront kings or national leaders about their sinful lifestyles and then prophesy about God's judgment upon their nation's wickedness and exercise supernatural powers of destruction to make my point, maybe I am not so interested.*

There are a couple of different ways to get your name before the people. The first is when your army defeats a great enemy and you return from battle a victor. The second is when you have to be the one who delivers the bad news to the nation or its leader and suffer a leader's rejection, condemnation from the populace, or both. If we knew that we could have the former and not the latter, we might be willing to take a double portion of our master's spirit. And if we had to choose the second option, then maybe greatness is not our real goal. Think about it for a moment and then decide after reading this example. Most of us do not go out and look for trouble by confronting people in sinful situations. Years ago I attended a training session in Nashville, Tennessee. After our meeting I was walking with a friend down Broadway toward Printer's Alley looking for a place to eat. As we walked and talked, we approached a man with a Bible in his hand, standing ready to speak to anyone who came out of a door about fifteen feet away. Suddenly to our left a man came out of an adult pornographic video store. The man with the Bible walked up to him and said, "Are you happy now that you have your belly and mind filled with filth? Let me tell you what God says about you." He started to read a passage of scripture. Before he could start the verse the other man pushed him down and ran down the street. My friend and I helped the man with the Bible up to his feet. He said, "I am all right," and then took up his place in front of the video store waiting for the next guy to come out. He looked at both of us and said, "If I only save one, it's worth it." We praised the man for his ministry. Then the two of us walked on discussing the scene we had just left. Both of us agreed that confronting men outside an adult video store was not our calling for ministry. But maybe God did call us and we were cowards and we wouldn't admit that we could confront that kind of sinner. You have to admire those who understand their calling so clearly that they are unafraid to confront the smallest evil or the greatest sinner in the world. Elijah had a baptism by fire with the prophets of Baal on Mt. Carmel. He may have had his fearful moments, but for most of his ministry he stood his ground and called men and women saint or sinner like he saw them. Elisha asked for a double portion of Elijah's spirit. Such a commitment if granted could easily have brought Elisha a horrendous death with terrible suffering. But Elisha asked anyway. The next fifty years of his ministry would not always bring him peace in a place where he could perform miracles and bring the dead back to life. But he was committed to carry out the work. Like the man with the Bible, even if he only saved one, it was worth it. Like all who accept the Lord's call to ministry there are moments when we understand clearly the hardship and difficulty that comes with the work, and we refuse to weasel out of those tough times. Thank God for those who have shown us the way of Christian service.

The call to achieve greatness by following in the footsteps of your predecessor is not as easy as it might seem. More than one aspiring leader has fallen on his or her sword trying to be their mentor's duplicate. More than one young minister has tried to be a Billy Graham and found out he wasn't. Each of us is created unique and different, yet all for God's purpose. Replicating yesterday's leadership styles and gifts may not work for the day or place where you serve. Not all gifts and styles can be learned and executed with the same skill and compassion as your mentor. Those who choose to follow great leaders soon find the road filled with demanding disciplines and a need for exceptional intuition and discerning wisdom. Here are some additional reasons why leadership, especially among God's people, is not so easy to achieve. First, there are those within the organization who may feel they are as capable as you are and should have been given this leadership position instead of you. Then there are those outside the organization who were in competition with you for the job and didn't get selected for your mentor's position either. Now they are angry and jealous over your selection and may take actions against your leadership. Finally, there are those who hated and despised your predecessor and now they will seize the moment to destroy and tear down all that he or she built and achieved before your selection. Oh! They are not angry with you unless you stand in the way of their mission to destroy your mentor's achievements. Understand that greatness often includes national or international recognition, power and material possessions. Ambitious people are always on the lookout for these positions. Not many will apply for the job in Nashville outside the adult video store confronting sinners on the sidewalk and taking what may come with the encounter.

Ahab called Elijah the "the troubler of Israel" (1 Kings 18:17, nasb). His view was probably based on more than just perception. It may have seemed to Ahab and Jezebel that every time they turned their hand to do something Elijah was in their face telling them they couldn't do it. Not many can take on the top leader single-handedly and survive. Ahab's words certainly expressed how he felt about God's prophet when he told Jezebel what Elijah had done and how he had killed her prophets with the sword. When she heard the news about her prophets she sent a message to Elijah saying, "So may the gods do to me and even more, if I do not make your life as the life of one of them by tomorrow about this time" (1 Kings 19:2, nasb). Such words were not an invitation for lunch written on expensive paper with a stamped R.S.V.P. inside a gold trimmed envelope. If she could have captured him, he would have been as dead as her prophets were. Who wants a job where people are ready to take your life if they can get their hands on you? Elisha was not blind or deaf to Israel's history. He knew Israel's political situation. It was only a few days or weeks after Jezebel's threat that Elijah found Elisha, the son of Shaphat, plowing with twelve yoke of oxen and threw his mantle over him. Elisha responded to this call by sacrificing a pair of oxen and giving the food to the people. Then he "arose and followed Elijah and ministered to him" (1 Kings 19:1–21, nasb). It took a brave, dedicated man to keep up with Elijah. And a double portion of his spirit would be needed if he were to take Elijah's place confronting sinners in the next generation.

Having the right qualifications for a job can be just as difficult as finding the right career of your dreams. Confucius supposedly said, "Choose the job you love, and you will never have to work a day in your life" (To Inspire, 2004). We must acknowledge that times were different back then. Most of what we know about Elisha's early life and background are found in 1 Kings 19. Scripture says he came from a wealthy family. Few families in Elisha's day owned one ox, let alone twelve pair. Elisha was no stranger to hard work. Managing a pair of oxen in the field is no simple task. Maybe he saw the call to follow Elijah as easier than working his father's fields. However, being raised in wealth and working hard in the fields are hardly the qualifications needed for confronting kings for their sinful behavior. And what qualifications were needed when God sent Elijah with a message to Ahaziah, Ahab's replacement, telling him he was wrong to inquire of Baal-zebub, the god of Ekron. "Now therefore thus says the Lord, 'You shall not come down from the bed where you have gone up, but you shall surely die'" (2 Kings 1:6, nasb). When Elijah's words got to King Ahaziah, he sent his captain and fifty men to bring him in. The first fifty men were consumed with fire from heaven and so were the second fifty the king sent. When the third captain was sent with fifty more, he begged Elijah to spare his life and come down and see the king. God spared the captain and his men, who brought Elijah before King Ahaziah to tell him that his death was imminent.

Elisha knew it would take a double portion of Elijah's spirit to be able to live under such tasks and responsibilities. Now, do not hear me saying that there are no benefits from following a great leader. There are good things that can be said also about Elisha wanting a second portion of Elijah's spirit. While successful people have their critics, they also have their supporters. No matter how much we may disagree with someone's theology, ethics, or morals, you cannot discount that their methodology enabled them to successfully sell themselves or their products. Let's think more about that for a minute because following successful people does have benefits.

The first is that working around people whose character and lifestyle demonstrate success establishes creditability. Some of your predecessor's success will rub off on you. Millions of people in this world crave success, yet they never will be successful because they do not have a clue or the vision about what it takes to be successful. They lack the drive and are unwilling to make the sacrifices necessary to achieve greatness. Let's go back to the man with the Bible on the street in front of the video store. Success for him was not wealth or becoming pastor of a large church. His goal was not to convert hundreds of men from pornography, but just one. If by hard work, sacrifice, and danger he could convert another one, maybe God would help him do it again and again until he closed the pornographic video store. That's success, maybe not by some people's standard, but it was by his. You must have a clear vision of what it takes to get to where you want to go and that requires some thinking first. Dr. Phil in his book *Life Strategies* says, "You have to name it to claim it" (McGraw, 1999). A clear picture of what you want shortens the time and resources needed to get from where you are to your goal. Most of us are not that clear about our own goals so our time and energy are spent helping someone else achieve their goals.

How you view your job and the words you use to describe it tell us more about who you are than the historical data does about your job. Your tone of voice, gestures, eye movements tell about your attitude, perception, and courage for the work you do. It is the same when you complain about your work. It tells the listener a lot about who you are and the quality of work you do. Dr. Charles Garfield once wrote an amazing story about a man and his perception about his work.

If you have ever gone through a tollbooth, you know that your relationship to the person in the booth is not the most intimate you'll ever have. It is one of life's frequent non-encounters: You hand over some money; you might get change; you drive off. Late one morning in 1984, heading for lunch in San Francisco, I drove toward a booth. I heard loud music. It sounded like a party. I looked around. There were no other cars with their windows open. No sound trucks. I looked at the tollbooth. Inside it, the man was dancing. "What are you doing?" I asked. "I'm having a party," he said. "What about the rest of the people?" I looked at the other toll-booths. He said, "What do those look like to you?" I pointed down the row of tollbooths. "They look like...tollbooths. What do they look like to you?" He said, "Vertical coffins. At 8:30 every morning, live people get in. Then they die for eight hours. At 4:30, like Lazarus from the dead, they reemerge and go home. For eight hours, (their) brain is on hold, dead on the job, going through the motions." I was amazed. This guy had developed a philosophy, a mythology about his job. Sixteen people dead on the job, and the seventeenth, in precisely the same situation, figures out a way to live. I could not help asking the next question: "Why is it different for you? You're having a good time." He looked at me. "I knew you were going to ask that. I don't under-stand why anybody would think my job is boring. I have a corner office, glass on all sides. I can see the Golden Gate, San Francisco, and the Berkeley hills. Half the Western world vacations here...and I just stroll in every day and practice dancing."

(Columbia South Carolina State Newspaper, 1999)

What does this story tell you about how you view your job? Perception is reality. Are you where you want to be because you view your work as a God-called opportunity to use your gifts? Or are you working for someone else, helping them achieve their goals, not your own? It is surprising that if you were to ask most people this question they would not have an answer, because they have never thought about it. They are just going through life day by day. And if they do think seriously about their job and career they would agree that they are not really happy because they are not using their gifts to achieve their own goals. Their work is just a job that pays the bills or buys the luxuries.

Elisha bonded with his master. He recognized that Elijah was not only a powerful man, he was God's man, voice, and agent to keep a nation and its leadership on a path toward spiritual holiness. He watched and listened. He discovered there was a difference between words men use and those Elijah used as he spoke for the Lord. Even though he came from a wealthy family, he learned that the Lord's people think differently. God's blessings on Elijah may not have been the kind Elisha expected for himself. Elijah's garments were not silk and wool, but dried leather animal skins. His food was the simple food of the poor. He dined out in the open, seldom in a house or temple. Yet his words were powerful and his message pure. All of us have choices about how and where we will live and work. Understanding where God wants you in his service and making a commitment to be God's person there takes courage and discipline. It is easy to fall into the belief that the world's standards for greatness, wealth, and luxury should be our standards. That is the message we see and hear every day. Then there is the other choice that usually doesn't end up with popularity, riches, and opulence. God's work is often hard, physically demanding, and materially unrewarding. Sometimes it may take a "double portion" of your predecessor's spirit to do the job, but God is ready to provide the resources if you are willing to answer the call. As Elijah came to the end of his days and ministry, he said to Elisha at Gilgal, "Stay here please, for the Lord has sent me as far as Bethel." But Elisha said, "As the Lord lives and as you yourself live, I will not leave you" (2 Kings 2:1–9, nasb). Elisha stayed with him until the end when he saw Elijah taken up to heaven; God rewarded him with the portion he asked for. Elisha took up Elijah's mantle that was left on the ground and started his new role as Israel's prophet. He asked for the job and he received the power to do the work. God gives us what we need to succeed if we center ourselves in his will. Elisha asked, "Give me a double portion of your spirit." Elijah said, "If you see me taken up you shall have it." Can you say that you wish you had said that? Maybe it isn't too late for either of us. Don't be afraid to ask. You might get what you ask for. Asking with the right words and following up with the right actions bring rewards that are out of this world.

For Further Bible Study

1. Contrast and compare the lives of these two prophets. How were they alike and how were they different? Dig deep and look for characteristics and behaviors worth emulating.

2. Discipleship often leads one to make hard choices about following the master teacher. Study the life of Stephen and his influence in Acts chapters 6 and 7, and verses 8:2, 11:19, and 22:20. Describe his dedication and what influence he had on others (Paul for example).

3. In your opinion is there a difference between Elisha and Stephen's willingness to follow their call to be a faithful servant no matter what the outcome?

For Personal Growth

1. The early church found many reasons to call men and women into God's service. Ask leaders of your church to help you research its history for men and women who were called into Christian work. Share your findings with your church when the right occasion is presented.

2. Was the layman with his Bible outside the adult video store a missionary, evangelist, both, or something else? Why or why not?

3. Go to your library or favorite bookstore and look for biographies of Christian leaders. Study their commitment and willingness to work in difficult circumstances. Look for similarities and differences between your call to service and theirs.

ESTHER SAID TO MORDECAI...

"IF I PERISH, I PERISH."

ESTHER 4:16

VIRTUOUS DECISIONS COME FROM THOSE WILLING TO ACCEPT VULNERABILITY.

One who is wise knows what to do. One who is trained knows how to do. One who is virtuous knows what is right to do. There is a big difference in these three. I wish I could say I always had the maturity and experience to know the right thing to do. Al Capone and Saddam Hussein were wise. They knew what to do by eliminating their competition and enemies. They trained their henchmen to know how to do their bidding, but what they did was not the right thing to do. While they may have been bold, cunning, and ruthless, they certainly were not virtuous. A virtuous decision is the most difficult decision to make because it calls for thinking at a higher level. I once attended a strategic planning seminar where George Bullard said, "A strategic thinker is a clock builder not just a time teller." (1996) Decision-making calls for strategic thinking. We must build our lives according to the right plan. We live, work, and play in a complex world where virtue in decision-making is not elevated to the level needed to make organizations, communities, and nations what they should be. For example, suicide bombers in Afghanistan, Iraq, Israel, Russia, and now in England and the United States believe sincerely in what they are doing. They believe that instant death to themselves, and unfortunately those who happen to be close to them, is a virtuous decision because it helps their group or cause to achieve its political or religious aim. They believe that their decision is right because their faith group interprets and approves it as a martyr's death. But how can there be virtue in a decision that provides power, wealth, or political advantage for one group and death and destruction to citizens of the same faith and nation?

Virtue in decision-making strives for moral excellence. Not because it is good for you or the disenfranchised, but good for everyone. This is why decision-making is so difficult. Achieving religious goals and aims does not necessarily mean that your decisions are virtuous. The Crusades were promoted as a virtuous and worthy endeavor. But the Crusades began with the wrong premise. Forcing ethnic or religious superiority over another culture that is deemed inferior is not a virtuous act. Destroying those who are different is a decision, but not a virtuous or morally sound one. Virtue is an acquired trait. We are not born with a desire to achieve what is virtuous. It is just the opposite. We are born with a desire to survive and overcome our enemies no matter what the cost or methods used. For most of us, life consists of repeated lessons learning how to deny self and make decisions for the benefit of our family, church, and community. Seldom is virtue a most sought after character trait because our perceptions differ so widely about what is true and right for every topic or issue. Ask two or three people what they think about anything and you usually have two or three differing opinions. Will our decision become virtuous because we believe them to be true or because they fit a narrow definition given to us by our faith group? If the majority agrees that our final outcome is a good one, does that allow us to justify the means we will use to achieve it? There is a lot to think about before coming to a simplistic stereotyped conclusion.

The problem with overly zealous orthodoxy and rigid leaders is that there is no room for ambiguity or those who disagree. For every question, issue, or problem there is only one right answer. This means that once a decision is made there is little room for improvement, change, and growth. The future is a repeat of the present. Those in power define truth. Joseph Stalin's purges could never fit even the broadest of definitions for a virtuous decision. To justify his claim to save the "motherland," he murdered thousands of Russians, Germans, Poles, Yugoslavians, Hungarians, and anyone else who stood in his way. Why? Because he defined the outcome he wanted, and those who disagreed with him were executed and lost their lives as enemies of the state. It is characteristic of despotic leaders to assume because they are top dog that their decisions are the right ones…and because they are right, for them, they must be virtuous for everyone else. For any behavior, if you are willing to search long enough, there is someone who can justify such action for you. When Moses returned from the mountain and found the Israelites making a golden calf he asked what happened. Aaron said, "You know how prone these people are to evil. They said to me, 'Make us gods who will go before us…So I told them, "Whoever has any gold jewelry, take it off." Then they gave me the gold, and I threw it into the fire, and out came this calf!'" (Exodus 32:22–24, nasb). How is that for quick thinking to justify your behavior? That happened more than 3,000 years ago. While we may not be able to duplicate what Aaron did to build a golden calf, we can come up just as many flimsy answers.

A more current example that is similar to Esther's predicament is when Zimbabwe's President Robert Mugabe replaced white farm owners with blacks in a controversial land reform initiative. It appeared to be an attempt to return land back to its original owners and provide poor blacks with an occupation that would boost their income and the nation's economy. His decision was interpreted and justified as virtuous by many third-world leaders. Thousands of white farmers were driven off their estates and hungry black Zimbabweans were resettled in their place. But his decision created an even deeper crisis. This created 300,000 unemployed farm workers, inflated prices more than 600%, and destroyed the country's economic agricultural base (Schwalm, 2007; Henderson-Blunt, 2007; *BBC News,* 2007). This is what happens when values and moral standards are compromised in order to place one ethnic group, ideology, or interpretation over another. Anarchy, rebellion, political, and economic unrest can be found all around the world today because greed and self-interest are placed as higher values. Virtuous decisions are sometimes very difficult to make.

Queen Esther found herself in just such a situation. King Ahasuerus promoted a man named Haman to serve as his senior counsel. In this position Haman advised the king that there was a certain group of people who were scattered in all the provinces whose guiding principles were different from those in the rest of the country. He suggested that since they did not observe the king's laws, it was not in the king's interest to let them live. He asked for the king to pass a decree that they be destroyed, indicating that he was willing to pay 10,000 talents of silver into the king's treasury to make it happen. What are the issues involved with Haman's proposal to exterminate the Jews? Were the

Jews uncooperative, failing to abide by the laws of the land? Haman certainly thought so. Was he correct in his perception? His anger was kindled against all Jews because a Jew named Mordecai refused to bow down to him and pay him homage as chief counsel to the king. In other words his ego and his feelings were hurt. Haman's solution to Mordecai's refusal to bow down was quick and easy. Just eliminate all the Jews. He was even willing to pay the king for the opportunity. The great Benjamin Disraeli once said, "Next to knowing when to seize an opportunity, the most important thing is life is to know when to forgo an advantage" (*The Week*, 2008).

When Mordecai discovered Haman's intention, he looked for a solution in Esther's relationship with the king. He felt if she could use her position it might keep the Jews alive. In my opinion he was no different than the wicked Haman who wanted to use his relationship with the king to get rid of Mordecai and the Jews. When Esther heard what was about to happen, she approached this situation differently. She called on her people to pray and fast…repent, seek God's face, commit themselves to the truth of God's leadership in their lives. Had she hurried to the king and entered his court without permission, she also may have been destroyed. Three days passed between the time she began to pray and fast and the banquet where she made her proposal to the king. In this interval the king had a night when he could not sleep. He had his servants read to him out of the book of records. In the history book was found an event concerning Mordecai that had not been completed to the king's satisfaction. Mordecai was rewarded. God's timing is always perfect, and we are rewarded when we wait for the right moment. No decision can be righteous or virtuous without consulting the Lord first.

Quick easy solutions sometimes work, but generally they are short-term fixes and often leave many issues unresolved or swept under the table with the hope that they will go away. Later these unresolved issues come back to haunt you. For some, fasting is a quick easy solution for a myriad of problems. The biblical view of fasting is that it should be taken seriously. Maybe that is the reason why fasting does not hold the high place for many in the Christian faith that it once did. Before Esther became queen she was a young woman named Hadassah, raised by her uncle, Mordecai. Because she was young and physically attractive she was taken into the king's harem. Her beauty and grace allowed her to rise to a position of prominence, replacing Queen Vashti. When Esther discovered Haman's wickedness against her ancestry, she began her search for a solution. She sent a message to Mordecai asking that all the Jews in Susa join her and her maidens in a fast for three days. Sometimes Christians feel they are too busy to fast or that fasting is really found more in the Old than New Testament. Fasting may be done for a variety of reasons. For some it is to deny themselves food or something desirable for a particular time to show humility, obedience, dedication, or commitment. For others fasting is a part of a program established by their church as a spiritual discipline. Esther chose to fast because the Jews' situation called for God's intervention. How, she did not know. So she started her decision-making process with prayer and fasting as a sign of her willingness to follow God's leading in this matter. With simple words "Go, assemble all the Jews…and fast for me," she committed herself to search for the right solution, not just a simple or easy victory over her enemy (Esther 4:16, nasb). Fasting calls for humility and a desire for the truth as it applies to our personal life. Esther knew that to approach the king for any reason when he had not asked for her to come into his presence could easily mean her death. Mordecai felt justified in making his case to Esther saying, "Do not imagine that you in the king's palace can escape any more than all the Jews. For if you remain silent at this time, relief and deliverance will arise for the Jews from another place and you and your father's house will perish" (Esther 4:13–14, nasb). Whose view and interpretation of this difficult situation was the right one: Esther's, Mordecai's, Haman's, the king's, or was there another view not yet discovered? Esther believed fasting would bring the right answer. It looks like she was right as future events turned out.

Clare Boothe Luce, abandoned by her father at age nine, became an author, playwright, social activist, politician, diplomat, and editor, once said, "Courage is the ladder on which all other virtues mount" (*Reader's Digest*, Wikipedia 2007). Hardship and difficulty can make or break anyone. Mordecai was desperate for himself and his people. He challenged Esther to be courageous. He believed that the right solution for the Jews' problem rested with Esther's ability to get the king to revoke his decree. This young Jewish woman met his challenge with courage saying, "If I perish, I perish" (Esther 4:16, nasb). She fasted and prayed, and God revealed to her that she should invite the king and Haman to a banquet. At the banquet she prepared herself for the right moment, and then after the king gave her the okay to make her petition, she humbly presented her case saying, "We've been sold, I and my people, to be destroyed…sold to be massacred, eliminated. If we had just been sold off into slavery, I wouldn't even have brought it up; our troubles wouldn't have been worth bothering the king over" (Esther 7:4, Msg.). Notice that she did not ask for her people to be removed from servitude, but only that they are allowed to live as servants within the kingdom. She was not asking for herself. Her only request was that they have the chance to live and serve the king. The king's anger was kindled, and he asked, "Who is he that would presume to do this?" (Esther 7:5, nasb). Esther identified Haman as the man. The king then realized that Haman had used his appointment to take advantage of the Jews. He decreed that Haman should die on the gallows he recently prepared for Mordecai's execution.

Simple words from Esther calling on her people to fast and pray for the right solution turned Haman's wicked and sinful decision around. Esther's courageous decision, "If I perish, I perish," shows a willingness to sacrifice her own situation for the needs of others. Such behavior exemplifies the sacrifice of our Savior who willingly went to Calvary's cross for us. We live in a complex, ambiguous world where changes that influence or affect our lives happen every day. How can we respond to such rapid changes unless we take time to ask God for his leadership? Self-sacrifice is generally not an option national leaders consider when making decisions that affect minorities, refugees, and the poor. It must be our first option for God's service. Prayer and fasting should not be overlooked when making important decisions.

There are five principles to help you live with the decisions you make in an ambiguous world. First, collect good data. Esther got her ducks in order before she went to see the king. Second, know what is happening and be informed. She sought God's leadership as to how to present her situation to the king without incurring his wrath. Third, have integrity to include what is best for all not just yourself. Esther sought what was good for the king and his kingdom while Haman sought what was good only for him. Fourth, practice love. Love conquerors a multitude of problems even before we begin looking for a solution to a problem. Love people, and together you can solve problems.

Finally, practice divine forgiveness. When we do make a mistake, we have a God who forgives our errors. If we will seek his face, he will forgive our mistakes. Our Lord admonished us to forgive others as we have been forgiven before we bring our gifts to the altar. A clean heart opens the door to the Lord's leadership.

Esther began with a good strategy that seems to have been a regular part of her daily living. This gave her courage and confidence that the Lord would guide future decisions as he had guided her past. Her words saved the Jews from destruction by a wicked man. Esther did not destroy Haman. He destroyed himself. There is virtue in decision-making when we seek God's face. One who is wise knows what to do. One who is trained knows how to do. One who is virtuous knows what is right to do. Esther found the right solution when she said, "…do not eat or drink for three days. I and my maidens also will fast in the same way…if I perish, I perish" (Esther 5:16, nasb). If virtue were easy to come by, we would live in a far better world with fewer problems. Since we have so many problems, we must look for better solutions before we waste our resources trying to destroy those who disagree with us. If we put our life on the line for the right reason we will find the best solution. "If I perish, I perish," she said. I wish I had taken more time to ask the Lord for a better solution before I made a decision to act, don't you?

For Further Bible Study

1. Are Jews and Christians the only people who fast? See Daniel 6:18.

2. How was Haman's anger against the Jews similar to Jezebel's anger against Elijah in 1 Kings 19?

3. Haman's plot against Mordecai is similar to what group of people who plotted against Daniel with the same results? (Daniel 6)

For Personal Growth

1. Can you remember a time when a person plotted against you or someone you know? What was the major reason(s) for the plot's success or failure?

2. In the situation above, was someone called in to rescue or to help look for a solution? Why were they chosen? Was it for their skills, gifts, spiritual life, life style, or resources?

3. When anger seems a quick choice for a situation, what method(s) do you use to make sure that your anger does not lead you into deeper difficulty? Is your method(s) something that can be shared or taught to another person?

SOLOMON SAID TO HIS SERVANT...

"GET ME A SWORD."

1 KINGS 3:24

WISDOM CAN BE MIXED WITH OTHER SKILLS AND ABILITIES.

Sometimes the crazier a story, the more interesting it is. This text begins with two women. One is either foolish or daringly audacious and courageous. The other is wise and humble. Two prostitutes come before Solomon, Israel's new king, and tell him their problem. Both had recently born children. One night one women's child died. Scripture tells us that the mother of the dead child got up and switched hers with the other woman's. When the mother of the living child awoke she discovered what had happened and asked for her child back, but the dead child's mother said, "No! For the living one is my son, and the dead child is your son" (1 Kings 3:22, NASB). Unable to sort this out, they are brought to Solomon for a decision. After questioning the two women, Solomon decided to cut the living child in two pieces and give half to each woman. The dead child's mother said it was okay to cut the living child in half if she couldn't have the whole child. The real mother, having compassion on her child, said no that she would give him up rather than watch him cut in half. From their answers, Solomon awarded the child to the right mother. This story is an example how values motivate people to make decisions and take extraordinary chances that may or may not turn out as they desire. One mother took a calculated risk to get up in the middle of night and switch her dead child for a living one even though she knew she was wrong. The other mother showed tremendous courage to be willing to give up her child rather than have him cut in half by Solomon's sword. It took wisdom for Solomon to believe that the Lord would lead him to make the right decision. While all three of them couldn't be right in this situation, they did make decisions that affected their futures. How do you know when you are making a wise decision that will turn out good for everyone involved? How do you know when your intuition is going to lead you to the right conclusion? Here are some thoughts that might help you.

Some years ago a woman attended a birthday party and saw a child that reminded her of what her child might look like six years after she supposedly died in a house fire even though there was no child's body discovered in the remains of the fire. For years this mother agonized over what had happened to her child. Now six years later at a child's birthday party she pretended the birthday child had gum in her hair and clipped off a lock. She later had it analyzed for DNA and compared it with her own. She discovered her suspicions were right. Her daughter had not burned to death in a house fire but had been stolen (Fox News, 2004). She turned her suspicions into a wise decision. How do you know when someone is bluffing pretending they are correct? Some people act with such assurance that you cannot tell by their actions when they are lying and when they are truthful. Solomon had no laboratory that he could call on to determine the DNA of the real mother and child. He was a new king. He may have had his own suspicions in this matter. What if he had been wrong? How much courage do you need to do what you know is right? Life is difficult enough to live when you are only making decisions for yourself. How much more complicated can it be when you include another person? It can really get difficult when that other person does not agree with your decisions and thinking.

In every presidential election we hear from each side claims about whose position is better on some issue. Are all candidates as wise and courageous as they say they are, or are they filled with ambition, self-interest, and false pride? John F. Kennedy in his book *Profiles of Courage* tells how Sam Houston masterminded the defeat of the Mexican army and captured the Mexican general, Santa Ana, making Texas independence possible. Houston became Texas' first president and later the first senator when Texas came into the Union. In 1854 Houston opposed the Kansas-Nebraska Act because it would nullify the Missouri Compromise of 1820 and 1850 by expanding slave holding states. The people of Texas opposed his decision, and he was defeated when he ran again for governor. When his term expired in the Senate he was called home. In 1859 he again ran and this time was elected governor. But when Texas voted to secede from the Union, he stood against the proposal and was relieved from his position as governor. It takes courage and wisdom as a politician to truly represent all your constituents when you know that your decisions may be seen as wrong in the eyes of many and right in the eyes of only a few.

Solomon asked God for wisdom, and the Lord granted it. But that example is only one moment in his life. There were times when he was not so wise and did not follow the Lord's guidance and leadership. The Lord never told him to marry foreign women nor make alliances with foreign nations or to carry out his father's wish and kill his enemies, but Solomon did it anyway. It is frightening to know that a nation's leader can be both wise and foolish. Of course we know that any leader is fallible. But would you trust the decision whether your son lives or dies to the wisdom of a new king whose wisdom had not yet been proven?

Each woman perceived Solomon's call for the sword differently. One was willing to sacrifice a child that was not hers so that the other woman could not have it. The real mother knew that she would rather give up the child she loved than have Solomon cut him in half. Giving up the child was hard but it was the right thing to do. All of us have been in a situation when we knew a decision we made was the right one, but it was not the one we wanted to make. How do you know when you are wise and not making a decision you will regret for the rest of your life? What if Solomon had accepted the other woman's willingness to destroy the child?

Was the woman whose child died wise when she stole the other woman's child and lied about it? No? What if she had gotten away with it? Would she then have been wise? In our culture we tend to give publicity and credence to people who do the wrong things and succeed. In some cultures a person is considered wise if they can lie, cheat, or steal their way to the leadership or wealth of the nation. Other mob members hold mafia crime bosses in high esteem. Friends and fans look acceptably on college athletes who cheat to stay eligible as long as they can win ballgames. Politicians who tell voters what they want to hear in order to gain reelection are viewed as politically wise and voter smart. Some Christians who parrot phrases and rhetoric that are based on faulty interpretations may think they are wise even when they know God hates a deceitful heart. Wisdom is not always identified by how loud and forceful you present your argument. Some of us know someone who has intelligence about a particular subject but whose lifestyle is indecent or is associated with criminals and lawbreakers. They may be wise but not about the right things. Proof of this is found in the growing number of movie stars, athletes, investment bankers, CEOs, and others who are convicted felons. Yes! They were smart enough to figure out how they could manipulate and take advantage of a situation for their own gain. But they were not smart enough to stay out of jail. Not all who are wise are righteous and holy in their living or lifestyle. The Apostle Paul talks about those who are wise in this world's wisdom, but foolish in the things of the spirit.

Naomi in the book of Ruth didn't see herself as worthy, so when she returned to Bethlehem, she had her old friends call her "Mara, for the Lord had dealt bitterly with her" (Ruth 1:20, nasb). Saul did not think it was wise on young David's part to go out to fight against Goliath without armor to protect him. And Rehoboam did not think it was wisdom that the elders gave him when they said he needed to be kind to Jeroboam and his people who wanted to have their load lightened. Jezebel didn't think Elijah was wise when he slew her prophets of Baal. Haman didn't believe Mordecai was wise in not bowing down to him when he passed by. People have not changed much since Bible days when these characters misinterpreted who was wise and who was foolish. Recently juries convicted famous stockbrokers of insider trading and did not think it was wisdom that led these men and women to take advantage of their positions as brokers, managers and owners. Instead they determined after the evidence was presented that it was criminal, and they were guilty of fraud and violating the law. The general public and newspaper editors did not think it was wise when journalists tried to create false news stories so that they could gain national fame. And so on and on it goes down through history when people decide it is okay for them to use their own position, money, perceptions, and standards to deceive the public for economic or political gain for themselves or their religious, ethnic, or political followers. Some even blame the Lord for their failures, saying, "The Lord told me to do it."

Solomon was considered wise because he had discernment to know who the real mother was. History will always look back on that moment as his wisest decision because it touches our hearts and points to one of our deepest concerns for a child's safety and well-being. Wouldn't it be a wonderful gift if we knew when we were wise and when we were not? We might then open or close our mouths only when we should, not just because we could. It is not easy to know when to ask for the sword and when to leave it alone. Take for example the fanciful story of the wolf, fox, and bear who went out hunting and bagged three deer (1993). Afterward they sat down and discussed how the spoils should be divided. The wolf said it was obvious that the only fair way was for each of them to have one deer. The bear promptly killed and ate the wolf. Then the bear asked the fox how the three deer should be divided. "You should have all three," said the fox. "Where did you get such wisdom," said the bear. "From the wolf," said the fox.

Some months ago, my Bible study guide called for me to begin looking at six Old Testament kings. I was asked to examine their leadership styles and to discover what skills, abilities, and talents they possessed that made them good or bad leaders for their people. Would those same qualities be the ones I should look for in the next political candidate running for my state or national office? There are voters who would disagree that using moral values and leadership styles found in scripture as a standard for public office is a good idea. Scripture teaches us that "The fear of the Lord is the beginning of knowledge; Fools despise wisdom and instruction" (Proverbs 1:7, nasb). There are those who think our president was wise when he sent troops to Iraq to depose a wicked, cruel dictator. Others are quite certain he was unwise and had other reasons and/ or agendas in order to gain some personal or political advantage. Regardless of what one believes about the president's decisions, the facts are that his wisdom or failure is more often determined by our own perceptions and interpretations surrounding an event. If things turn out well, then he is considered to have the skills, abilities, and talents that make one wise. If things do not turn out as some desired, then the leader is self-serving and motivated by greed or a political agenda.

I hope a sword will not always be considered as right method for settling a dispute, even though Solomon's bluff was successful. Saddam's bluster and bluff kept his neighbors nervous and the international community upset. Yet he kept using words that gave courage to his supporters that they could win a second war with the United States. Pictured with his many weapons for war, he held up the sword as a symbol of power and might. Solomon's father, David, was a powerful king of Israel and a mighty warrior. His major goal in life was to build a temple for the Lord, but he was denied such an opportunity when Nathan the prophet came and said there was too much blood on David's hands to build God's temple. Yes! There are those who win with the sword, but more often than not it is a foolish choice. Paul never appealed to the Corinthians to take up the sword against one another as a solution to their differences. He asked them in 1 Corinthians 13 to love, not destroy, their enemies. Jesus said to Peter after he struck the servant in the garden with his knife, "Put your sword back in its place, for all who draw the sword will die by the sword. Do you think I cannot call on my Father, and he will at once put at my disposal more than twelve legions of angels?" (Matthew 26:52–53, nasb). The wise consider all the options and choices before choosing to use or not use the sword.

Who then is wise and how shall we know wisdom

when we see it? Our Lord tells us that we can be wise and miss out on truth. Matthew 11:25 says, "I praise thee, O Father, Lord of heaven and earth, that Thou didst hide these things from the wise and intelligent, and didst reveal them to babes" (nasb). How can we be wise and not heed the words of Jesus? Maybe taking up our cross is a better choice than the sword. Paul adds in Romans 1:22, "Although they claimed to be wise, they became fools" (nasb). So it must be possible to claim wisdom and still not understand what is needed to make the right decision. Why is this truth so difficult for so many national leaders and politicians to grasp? Often it is selfishness and greed that gets in the way and overrides the wise decisions. Those Enron executives were at the top of the food chain feeling it was wise to falsify their company records and raise the value of their stock. But now one by one they are being convicted and losing their homes and fortunes and maybe spending the remainder of their lives in jail for their decisions. Their foolish decisions will never be forgotten by those whose retirements and life savings were destroyed in the fall of the company. *Newsweek* carried an interesting article by Dirk Johnson titled, "Policing a Rural Plague" about methamphetamine labs. The article stated, "In the past year police busted more than 9,300 meth labs nationally...a 500% increase since 1996" (2004). Many are wise enough to know how to make meth, but so foolish to believe that they can keep from getting caught and destroying their lives and almost everyone they touch. How hard is it to think you are wise when you are not? Judging by the increasing numbers in our state and federal prisons, it must be easier than some people might think. Sadly most felons do gain more knowledge after having been in jail for a while. But their knowledge seems limited to ways to commit criminal behavior and not get caught.

In an article entitled "Double-talk Fools Experts," Rob Warden tells about a lecture that was pure nonsense. The speaker was introduced as Dr. Myron L. Fox and identified by an ambiguous, high-sounding title. He was said to be an authority on the application of mathematics to human behavior. His subject was "Mathematical Game Theory as Applied to Physical Education." Actually, he was an actor hired by three medical educationists to prove a point. He fooled fifty-five educationists, school administrators, psychiatrists, psychologists, and social workers. Not one of them realized it was a hoax. One did say the presentation was too intellectual (Source Unknown). Any one of us in that same situation might have just as easily been conned into believing something that was not true. Was the audience wrong because someone unknown took advantage of them? Or were they self-serving to believe they were right in their own judgments about the speaker and the topic? In Solomon's case he had a discerning mind and developed a strategy to deal with two stories, one true and the other false. It was only in his decision to cut the living child in half that helped him to discern which explanation was true and the other false.

Every society has individuals who seem to lack the wisdom needed to keep them from making bad decisions. We live in a world filled with ambiguity and misinformation, and it seems to be getting worse, not better. In the cartoon strip *b.c.*, someone is always climbing to the mountain top to get advice from the Guru who is sitting at the top meditating. Most of the time the *b.c.*'s Guru gives information that is already available, turns out to be humorous, or wasn't worth all the effort to climb the mountain to get. So how would you help those seeking wisdom find real truth that would make them better people and this world a better place? How about Paul's words in 1 Corinthians 13 for a starting place?

Learn the skills needed for discerning truth from lies and excuses for bad behavior. "Dr. Charles Snyder, professor of clinical psychology at the University of Kansas, calls excuses social lubricants that encourage people to take chances" (1990). As long as we are willing to believe lies and excuses are acceptable behavior people will continue to give them to us. Often military leaders will teach new recruits in basic training to say, "No excuse, sir," when they do something wrong. I think the idea behind this is to teach a new recruit that he/she is responsible for their actions and behavior, so no excuse is needed nor will one be accepted. The two prostitutes came before King Solomon with different stories about how this event transpired. Obviously one was lying, but which one?

Sometimes life is dangerous or filled with difficult and conflicting choices. Making the right decision requires gathering information and drawing on experiences sometimes a person does not have or is unable to gain in time. Gaining wisdom is a life-long process that never ends. So how can you survive in a world filled with ambiguity and misinformation? If we are always willing to seek the truth and apply the lessons we learn from our own mistakes and the failure of others, we will make better decisions. Solomon's request for wisdom was evidenced by his willingness to trust the Lord by faith. Then his decision to call for a sword turned out well because it revealed the true mother. Wise decisions honor the Lord.

For Further Bible Study

1. Which commandments did the woman whose child died break? (Exodus 20:1–17)

2. Can you think of the name of an Old Testament prophet who brought a mother's child back to life because of her faith? (1 Kings 8:4–50)

3. Solomon is known for his wisdom, but he also made many foolish decisions too. What decisions in your opinion hurt his reputation the most? (1 Kings 11)

For Personal Growth

1. Our parents, relatives, and friends have often warned us of the dangers of giving our heart to ungodly causes. Can you make a list of some dangers you avoided and others you did not? Is there something in either of these lists you need to work on now?

2. Sometimes people who are very wise and deeply spiritual are resented, abused, or persecuted. Can you think of an example? How well do they handle rejection?

3. Who is someone you know who has godly wisdom? Research his or her life and lifestyle and see if you can find the answer to why his or she is a person whom many people look to because of wisdom.

NEHEMIAH SAID TO THE WORKERS...

"DO NOT BE AFRAID."

NEHEMIAH 4:14

FEAR FAILS WHEN FAITH IS A FACTOR.

In 1933 Franklin Roosevelt at his first inaugural address as president said, "The only thing we have to fear is fear itself." Many of those fears and questions facing Americans in those early Roosevelt years are similar to the Jewish exiles making preparation for their return from Babylon to Jerusalem back in 538 BCE. Both faced an uncertain future about what tomorrow might bring. No matter what the time or season, uncertainty makes us uncomfortable. Some types of uncertainty create fear for you while the same uncertainty for others brings laughter or unconcern. And what about those who say they are never afraid of anything? Are they truly honest with themselves? When I was training to become a paratrooper I was never anxious about jumping out of an airplane. My acrophobia (fear of heights) came weeks earlier when I was learning how to jump out of a thirty-four-foot tower strapped in a harness and hooked to a cable to keep me from hitting the ground. Once I conquered the fear of falling out of the tower I knew I had the skills and courage to jump out of an airplane. There are many kinds of fear, maybe more than you want to know about. Here are a few unusual ones: hypergyophobia—fear of taking responsibility; neophobia—fear of new things of what will happen next; chronophobia—fear of growing old; kikephobia—fear you'll get what you deserve; thanatophobia—fear of death; triskaidekaphobians are those who fear the number 13; cyberphobians fear computers; and probably the worst one, paniphobia—fear of everything (Mufson, 2006).

Feeling fearful is a normal natural behavior. Our minds know how to deal with fear. Malcolm Gladwell in his book *Blink* (2005) tells us that in the time it takes for us to blink our eyes, our mind has offered us choices for dealing with fearful events. The usual choice is, do you want to run away or stay and deal with this situation? Sometimes the mind reminds us, *You have not been in this exact situation before, but here are similar situations. Do you want to evaluate any of them?* If we decide we want to stay and deal with the dangerous situation confronting us, then our brain starts getting our body ready to respond. Messages are sent out from the brain to organs and tissues to prepare us for the action we plan to take. Hopefully our minds will bring up the right solution to our needs. Fear must be put into the proper perspective and be dealt with by looking carefully at all the facts and information needed to help us choose the right response. Creating imaginable fears in people to lead them to make the wrong decision is a tactic that has been used for centuries. Calming people to release their fear and make the right decision has been the role of leaders like Roosevelt and Churchill during World War II.

The prophet Nehemiah might have found President Roosevelt's words a useful phrase to encourage the exiles during their journey back to Jerusalem. Most of the Jewish exiles under Zerubbabel, Ezra, and Nehemiah may have had high exhilaration and enthusiasm about returning to Jerusalem from their exile in Babylon. Some others may have had mixed emotions, even fear, about coming back to their national homeland. The exile took place over a period of seventy years (Jeremiah 29:10–14, nasb). The Babylonians had destroyed Jerusalem in 597 BCE. Now under Cyrus, the Persian, they were being told to go home and start a new life. But some may have wondered with what and how. Questions were proposed and considered from a variety of viewpoints during the long journey to Jerusalem. A destroyed city required engineers, carpenters, and stonemasons. Where would they be found? For a few exiles each step toward the unknown in Jerusalem took them away from the security they had know in Babylon. Who or how would they be protected? For others, their enthusiasm was not without some fear and trepidation about what to expect when they arrived. Leaving Babylon for the unknown ahead in Jerusalem increased their anxiety and added a new burden about their future. How long would it take to rebuild the walls so they would be safe at night? With a little money, clothing, and a few pieces of furniture, they bravely entered the city and their new home. The young and old, foreign or native born Jerusalemites had lots of questions as they faced the difficulties surrounding the rebuilding of the city. Could they do it themselves? What if they couldn't? Who could they call on for help? Was all this effort a gigantic mistake? Exiles, who had never known Jerusalem's past grandeur, were overwhelmed by the city's destruction and poverty when they arrived. For those who were born and raised in Babylon one question could have been, *Why would anyone want to return to a city that is in this condition?*

Their fears remind me, somewhat of my own, when I was assigned to the 101st Airborne Division at Fort Campbell, Kentucky, where I met and married my wife. No longer single, I could not bring her to live with me in the barracks. So I rented a sparsely furnished apartment one week before leaving to get married. On the way back after a short honeymoon and just twenty-three years old, I began to wonder if maybe I had taken on more responsibility than I could handle. I had good friends, belonged to a great church, and had a steady job…more than many who married at my age, but would it be enough? Looking back now, many years later, like most people I realize I had some unfounded fears about all that was involved in setting up house-keeping. Thanks to my new bride, our friends, our parents, and our strong work ethic, we survived. Those Jewish exiles, returning to Jerusalem, had a lot more issues to face with a lot less resources than I had. Their faith, raw courage, and determination helped them start out on a new adventure. Believing God's chosen leaders would work out the details, they departed Babylon for a new home and freedom to determine their own destiny.

"Don't be afraid," are words most of us have said to ourselves or heard from someone else say many times. Nehemiah discovered upon their arrival in Jerusalem that it was in ruins and unpopulated (Hamrick, 1970). The first thing he did upon his arrival in Jerusalem was to make a secret inspection of the ruined walls. He discovered the walls were in terrible condition, making the city vulnerable to enemy attack. In addition, there was open outspoken opposition from their Samaritan half-relatives within and outside the city who were determined to make rebuilding the walls even more difficult. It must have been a depressing sight for Nehemiah to see Solomon's temple and the city's walls destroyed. He must develop a plan quickly for the defense of the city lest their life and purpose would be destroyed.

God had chosen him as their leader because he was a man of vision. Success depends on when and where resources are used and energy is focused. There was the immediate need for trust and security. He told them, "Do not be afraid of them; remember the Lord who is great and awesome, and will fight for your brothers, your sons, your daughters, your wives and your homes" (Nehemiah 4:14, nasb). He must come up with a plan for feeding those who worked on the walls and could not plant gardens or raise food for their families. His words soon empowered the people with a plan that challenged them to get busy.

It is important to remember that bad leaders can use similar words to motivate people to achieve their own goals. In this passage the exiles are motivated by Nehemiah, whose major goal is to reestablish God's leadership over his people in the holy city the Lord gave them under King David. But, it was in this same city that Absalom used words to motivate the people against his father, King David. David was forced to flee the city until his army could be gathered to take it back. For all his words Absalom failed in his effort to overthrow his father and in the end was slain in battle by Joab, the commander of David's army. Whatever similarities there were in the words David, Absalom, and Nehemiah used, one thing is certain: each person understood those words differently and responded for different reasons and purposes. That is why it is so difficult to get people to agree definitively on a definition for any word. "Be not afraid" meant something different to Absalom's rebel army, Joab's trained forces, and Nehemiah's refugees coming back from Babylon. We define words according to our own experiences—seldom according to someone else's. Therefore, there are few words or topics any two people will totally agree upon as the only definition. Usually we will accept something close enough to carry on the conversation or complete the task. However, when we disagree about a word's meaning, the trouble starts.

Nehemiah first rebuilt the walls, then the city. The legal and political reforms that were established during this period came after the exiles' confidence had been restored by their successes in rebuilding the walls and the city. When the exiles felt secure, fears were abated; they began to build their own homes and places to work to conduct business. Then they could turn their attention to other less important matters. Feeling secure is one basic requirement for every nation. Part of any successful endeavor in overcoming fear is to focus on the right priorities and carefully utilize your resources wisely. Fear is seldom a problem when you are focused on projects that interest you. By concentrating on the project or work at hand, you eliminate the debilitating fears that destroy your self-confidence. Annually, around the world millions of people are immobilized by fear. While their mind is offering suggestions, choices, and options, they are rejecting them and focusing on the fear instead of a solution.

When faced with threats from more than one source, a bird will often preen its feathers and seemingly wait for the doom to come. In a similar fashion, we are sometimes so paralyzed by fear that we perform irrelevant or illogical actions that do not help the situation at all (making a bed, pacing the floor, etc.). Such a coping mechanism is maladaptive and emotion-focused and does not contribute to the successful resolution of the fearful situation (Folkman & Lazarus, 1980; Zeitlin, 1980).

Think with me for a moment about a university's basketball game. Suppose there are 36,000+ fans in the arena, the score is tied and the home team has committed a foul. The opposing team's player steps up to the foul line and 30,000 fans start shouting and waving things to distract him. If he makes the free throw it will be because he focused on the task before him rather than the score or the home team fans distractions. Military personnel are trained to the same standard of behavior. If they do their job and it meets or exceeds the standard, they have done what they were trained to do. A swarm of enemy in superior numbers may be a few hundred yards away, but if the friendly forces are focusing on doing the job at hand, they can defeat three to five times their opposing force. When a foundation is laid, if it is off by only an inch, the building will not be true. Everything else built on top of it will have to be adjusted, shortened, or lengthened. Faith in yourself, faith in your co-workers and your leaders drives away fear and puts you in the winner's circle. Laying the right foundation helps eliminate fear to build on it. A *Time Magazine* article recently said, "While most golfers can't believe they won, Tiger Woods sounds like he expected to win or can't believe he didn't" (2001). Fear destroys your faith in yourself and the task that is before you. Removing fear gives you the ability to focus your energy and resources on the problem and results in the better decisions.

George Bullard, in a meeting I attended in South Carolina, used an example from Charlie Brown who was busy pasting stamps in a book. "Oh!" said his sister, Sally, "I see you have taken up a hobby collecting stamps." Charlie Brown said, "Oh! Is that what it is? I thought I was just supposed to keep busy" (Bullard, 1996). Clergy do a lot of spiritual planning and lots of busy work, but little strategic preparation. The opposite of planning your options is crisis management. And heaven knows preachers do enough of that. What could we do if we had a plan and let our church buy in on it as they were empowered? It is true that the exiles' enemies were outside and within the city. It was also true that the task required untold resources that would not be discovered until the work began. But Nehemiah was responsible for these issues and more as their leader. The exiles were responsible for following his leadership and dedicating themselves to the task he assigned them. Build the walls…two foot high, then eight, then twelve and twenty until they were high enough to keep their enemies out. Starting with the right priorities and a plan to get going, the exiles headed in the right direction. You can make changes as you need to, but without a plan and a priority list, the probability of success becomes more doubtful. Nehemiah had a plan and called on the exiles to execute his plan. In doing so they had to focus on the task before them. Rebuild the walls first, and by getting the walls done, they were able to enjoy shelter safe inside the city day or night should an enemy attack them. Planning is the key to success. This project was what they needed to move from fear to faith. Nehemiah's word that God had taken care of their brothers and families in the past was good advice. Why not assume that he will continue to do so now for the work that was to be done? Rebuilding the walls was not busy work. Planning, like faith, eliminates fear. Planning can take many names and/or approaches: strategic, retirement, long-range, debt-reduction, income generating, and on and on it goes. But without a plan, which direction is best? What resources are needed? A good motto is "Plan your work and then work your plan." I often advise people in counseling who are having problems getting things done to sit down each morning and ask the Lord, "What should I do today?" Then make a list of things to do. Prioritize the list, and then thank the Lord for the strength and resources he will provide for you today to get those things done. If everything on your list does not get a high priority, then move them to another day. Then you are certain that the most important items are done first and in the right order so the rest can follow in a logical sequence. You will discover your fears are calmed; you will feel better and rest well at night when the important things are done and behind you.

Nehemiah offers us the same suggestion today. Focus on the tasks that God gives us each day and let tomorrow take care of itself. If we do God's work one day at a time, we will never be afraid of what the future will bring because our Lord was with us yesterday and today and will be with us tomorrow. His blessings, love, and grace do not end when the sun goes down like the ancients who believed their god died each evening and was resurrected on the next morning. Scripture says, "Behold he who keeps Israel will neither sleep nor slumber" (Psalm 121:4, kjv).

Often today physicians will prescribe diet and exercise as a solution to a multitude of physical and emotional problems. Why? Because studies have found that if you are doing something good for your mind and body or someone else, it has an overall good effect on decreasing anxiety and fear in your mind. Focusing on the goals and tasks Nehemiah set before them, the exiles found they were just the right words for an anxious group needing a successful start. Next time you find yourself in a dilemma, try to remember those exiles walking back from Babylon on the long, hot, and dusty roads, all the while fearfully turning each bend in the road wondering what difficulties would face them when they arrived in Jerusalem. Nehemiah had it right. "Do not be afraid...remember the Lord is great and awesome" (Nehemiah 4:14, nasb). Trust the Lord and get started on something good. When someone I know is immobilized by fear, maybe I should remind him or her of Nehemiah's situation: "Do not be afraid." Faith overcomes fear. I hope I can say that next time.

For Further Bible Study

1. In Joshua 1, what advice did he give to his people concerning their present fears?

2. What advice does Jesus give us in Matthew 6 for dealing with daily fears and anxiety?

3. Do a study on one or all of the following Bible characters: King Saul, (1 Samuel 13), Gideon, (Judges 6:33–40), or Gehazi, (2 Kings 5:20–27). What were they anxious or fearful about? Did their anxiety and fears add to their problems or help them find the right solution?

For Personal Growth

1. Choose three of your friends who seem to have a lot of self-confidence. Ask them to tell you how they handle fears and anxieties when confronted

with difficult situations. What can you learn from their responses to build your own self-confidence?

2. Stress is often called "the silent killer." Search the Internet and make a list of illnesses that can result from unrelieved stress? Do you think stress reduction is worthy of your attention and effort? If you discover stress reduction is needed, what is your plan to relieve your stress?

3. Was Jesus ever anxious or stressed? When? How did he deal with his situation?

ELISHA SAID TO THE PROPHET'S WIFE...

"GET MANY VESSELS NOT A FEW."

2 KINGS 4:1–7

YOUR SUCCESS SOMETIMES DEPENDS ON SOMEONE ELSE'S HELP.

It is probably a true saying that everyone who is or was successful had help from someone along the way. Dr. Billy Graham's success could be attributed to the Hearst family newspaper's effort to "puff Graham." While some might argue that God had a purpose for Dr. Graham's ministry that goes beyond the newspaper's coverage of his crusade, it certainly didn't hurt his ministry to have the national press coverage that he received. Sometimes it is inspiring as well as surprising to make a list of people from whom you have received guidance, instruction, and/or training over your lifetime. How about those who helped you restore your self-confidence, listened to your complaints, patched up your broken heart, and helped you build your dreams? Before we move on, how about those who supported you, gave you the resources you needed, and backed you up when you wanted to quit? Do any of us really want to make the claim that we are totally self-made persons and got where we are on our own? I wouldn't think so. I know I had a lot of help.

I was never much of a student in high school. I had other interests in sports and an active social life that took preference over my studies. About 90% of my high school's graduates enroll in a college or university…even if they only attend for a semester or two. In my senior year, my English teacher, Mrs. Mary Hartwick, asked me what my plans were after graduation. "Frankly," I said, "I don't have any." She gave me an application for her small Presbyterian college in Alma, Michigan. They accepted me, but I only attended for three semesters before I flunked out and joined the army. I guess my priority was that I still wanted an active social life more than spending time in classes or studying. But I was headed in the right direction from that moment in her high school classroom when she helped me get into college. There were others who encouraged me too. Rev. Robert Gaultney was my youth pastor. He gave me a couple of opportunities to speak in churches, and I enjoyed the experience. You see, we never know what people and events will influence our future. There is a right moment in time when someone or something changes the direction our life is taking. It was that way with me when my church basketball coach led me to Christ. It was that way when a West Point officer challenged me to follow up on my earlier preaching experiences. Those influences helped me risk moving beyond my own interest in sports and dating girls to a higher calling and a more challenging lifestyle. I look back on those who had an influence on my life and I see Christian ministry all throughout the process. They were just sharing what they had experienced as a Christian to help me find the right pathway. There is an old story about a young monk who followed St. Francis of Assisi around through the alleys and streets of the city. He finally asked, "When are we going to preach?" "We have been," replied Francis. "We have been seen and watched by people as we walked, and it is no use to preach unless your walk is an example of your preaching" (*Our Daily Bread,* 1991). Some of the greatest help I experienced didn't come from a pulpit. It came from the words people spoke in my classrooms, or on the fields where I played football, baseball, and ran track. Sometimes wisdom came from friends like Chief Warrant Officer Don Maloney and Specialist Carl Bennett's wisdom while we ate meals together and discussed careers, lifestyles, and growing up.

The books of 1 and 2 Kings are filled with wonderful vignettes where one Bible character's life and career influenced another person through some life-changing event. These simple short stories tell us in a few words what made the difference between success and failure, change and redundancy in someone's life. Our scripture passage here is such an example. Tragedy struck the home of a widow and her two sons. Unable to make ends meet, the widow borrowed money from creditors and when the time came she couldn't repay her debt. She went to the Prophet Elisha and said, "The creditor has come and is threatening to take my two sons as slaves for payment" (1 Samuel 4:1, nasb). This widow was not the first to discover that her good intentions only left her deeper in trouble. Nor would she be the first to discover that the right solution to her problem, when properly executed, would change a crisis into a victory and a wonderful end to the story. Almost everyone knows at least one person whose life was changed from failure and defeat into a successful life-changing career because someone gave them a little help. Second Kings 4 contains at least three such wonderful stories where a crisis is turned into great victory. Check out these wonderful life-changing stories and see for yourself.

The widow's story began with a crisis. In desperation she went to the prophet Elisha and asked for help. His reply was interesting. He asked, "What do you have in the house?" The widow listened carefully and her mind raced through the library of resources that once were a part of her home, but they were no longer available. She checked for bread, and her mind replied, *Gone.* She asked herself if there was meat, flour, or any other food resource. The answer came back again, *Gone,*

gone, and gone. Then she remembered this morning as she went to the cupboard for food to feed her sons she found among a few dishes a small flask of oil. So to the prophet's question, the widow replied, "Nothing except a flask of olive oil" (1 Samuel 4:2, n a sb). If I were telling the story as if it were happening today the widow would know that there are many places in her city where she might go for assistance. Food pantries, rescue missions, women's shelters, etc., all might have the resources she wants and needs. However, she couldn't choose those. Instead she must go to her church and talk to the pastor for whom her husband worked. Churches for thousands of years have been a place of refuge for the poor and needy.

But our story does not end with aid and comfort from the church or any other charity. Here is where that story today differs from the one in 2 Kings 4. Relief would not be found in a storeroom, warehouse, or government agency buildings. The prophet tells her in so many words that she is going to have to work for it. For a few poor today these words would not be good news. Handouts are acceptable, laboring for food staples doesn't always agree with their perception of how this crisis should be handled. I often ask those who are requesting help and assistance from our church for food or to pay for a water, electric, or rent bill that has come due, "If our church were able to help you, what would you do next week or next month when this crisis occurs again?" Specifically, I am looking for an answer that says they try to live on a budget or they have employment coming in a few days and that this crisis is only temporary or until they find work. If they are unable because of illness or a handicap I try to find out if they have used federal, state, or local government resources to provide help over the long term because our church is not financially able to help over a long term. In some cases I have found callers not interested in work, but prefer to stay at home and use the telephone to ask for help and assistance. Of course they are depressed and in need of assistance, but more often than not it is their lifestyle and attitude that is keeping them in this crisis. I belong to a strong mission church committed to helping where we can. Like Elisha we expect the caller to use what resources God has already given them to provide for themselves. Elisha asked her what she had, and she responded with "only a flask of oil" (2 Kings 4:2, nasb). He asked her to start with what she had.

Miracles more often than not begin with who you are and or where you are. What is at hand and available is usually more important than expecting solutions to drop out of the sky. In his book *90 MINUTES IN HEAVEN*, Don Piper covers his terrible automobile accident that took him from life to death and back to life again. He starts off Chapter 14 saying, "Some things happen to us from which we never recover, and they disrupt the normalcy of our lives. That's how life is" (2004). And he is absolutely correct. We are never the same again after the Lord brings change and miracles like these into our life. I like stories about some poor widow who finds that a deacon or friend has brought a couple of bags of groceries and enough coal to get her through the winter. Sometimes such stories seem impossible. The television program *MacGyver* was built on the ingenuity of MacGyver's wisdom to use what was at hand to escape the crisis. The program's writers scripted MacGyver's miracles just as God provides ours. But after the event we are never the same. In the widow's situation people today would be tempted to think, *Are you crazy? One small flask of oil is going to feed three people for the next few weeks, month, or years?* Yes, miracles happen in this old world every day. MacGyver's program, Don Piper's trip to heaven and then back to earth, and this poor widow's miracle flask of oil, all start with who is willing to help and what is available to be used for the Lord's glory.

Our widow, after visiting the prophet, returned home to her two hungry teenagers who were hoping she had burgers, fries, and a shake or soft drink in a bag from the local fast food restaurant. No such luck. She told her hungry sons that their pastor had suggested that she borrow empty pots and pans from the neighbors and fill them with oil from the flask. One son looked at the other, rolled his eyes, turned to his mother, and said, "Mom, you aren't serious, are you? This is crazy!" But she was adamant and would not be discouraged, sending the two boys out to the neighbors to borrow as many pots as they can. Now I know how

I acted and behaved as a child and teenager when it came to work. But I also knew that I had better follow Mom's directions. Like most boys I wouldn't travel down the street to a house that was the farthest away to start borrowing pots and pans until I had all I could carry. Most young men would begin as I would, with the house next door to mine and get a few, hoping they would have enough. Do you suppose that it was probably the same with these two boys? They brought home the empty vessels but not enough. Each time she sent them out again they had to travel farther until she grew weary of their complaints and said, "Okay," and she shut the door. Then she took the first pot or pan and began pouring the oil, and the miracle began. The pot slowly filled, and there was still more oil in the flask. "Amazing," said one of the sons as he handed her a second vessel. Her other son set the vessel aside. This went on for some time, and the widow said, "Give me another vessel." Her son responded that they were all filled and no empty vessel was left. Suddenly the oil stops coming out of the flask, and the task was completed. She followed instructions exactly as the prophet gave them to her and it worked.

The widow returned to the prophet and told him about the miracle and the full vessels all around the room. Elisha was pleased. He said, "Go sell the oil and pay your debts and you and your sons can live on the rest" (1 Samuel 4:7, n a s b). And she did that as quickly as she could, not only redeeming her sons from the hands of the creditor, but using funds left over to feed her boys until work was available. What a happy ending. We like stories like this because they tell us that God will provide. The story also tells us that if we are faithful and obedient good things can happen. May I suggest that there is a simple detail often unnoticed that makes this story even more exciting? Because I know myself and know what it was like to be young and a poor kid raised in a wealthy town, I think I understand something about how the young boys' minds worked when their mother suggested they go to the neighbors and borrow empty vessels, not a few. For example, one of the chores my parents gave me and my brother was to carry out the trash and ashes from our coal furnace and put them at the curb for pickup every Monday morning on our way to school. Almost without fail at the supper table every Monday night my father would ask if we had completed our task. So it wasn't something we could forget or get out of easily. Being typical boys we did only what we were told. We carried out what was in the containers…nothing more. If boxes or trash were stacked up on the ground beside the container, we felt that was someone else's responsibility unless were told specifically something else had to go out with the trash. Ours was to take that container up the stairs and out to the street where it could be picked up and taken to the dump. Is it safe to say that most boys between eight and sixteen do not get too excited about work? I hate to judge others by myself, but a boy's attitude is something my brothers and I knew something about. Especially if it kept them from doing things they wanted to do instead of working.

Now back to the widow. How much oil did she have to sell to pay her debts? We do not know except to say that the scripture tells us it was enough to pay her debts and enough left over to support her two sons. The unnoticed detail here is that she had enough left over to support herself and her two sons. Apparently the sons brought enough vessels to do the job and provide an abundance left over. But what if they had been slovenly in their duty? What if the boys complained they were tired and unable to get any more? Would the widow, tired of cajoling and begging the boys, have allowed them to quit with only a few vessels? Sure that might have happened. But...The opposite might be true also. What if the boys had brought ten or twenty or fifty vessels? Would God have filled all the pots and pans the boys brought? Yes! And here is the principle to remember: God's blessings are often tied to our faith and obedience as good stewards of our time and resources. The more faithfully we exercise tasks (getting pots and pans for oil) without being greedy, the more blessings we can receive. Jesus said that if we had "the faith of a grain of mustard seed," we could move mountains (Luke 17:6, nasb). But there is more to miracles that a little faith. Sometimes God waits for us to stimulate our faith with action, obedience, and good stewardship. Apparently the two boys brought a sufficient number of vessels. The scriptures tell us that Elisha told her to pay her debts and live on the rest. I am not emphasizing greed here. It does not seem to be Elisha or God's intention for the widow to live in luxury and wealth for the rest of her life from this simple miracle. But Elisha's instruction to live on the remainder after her debts were paid is certainly tied to the number of vessels the boys borrowed from their neighbors. It seems as if the woman and her sons paid attention to details.

Therefore, success comes easier when we listen carefully to the wisdom and advice God gives us. Is it your habit to listen carefully to the instructions you are given? Most of us think we understand but fail to get all the data and amounts in the correct order and then wonder why the directions, repair, recipe, or result is a failure. The widow listened carefully and followed Elisha's instruction. Did the boys do as well carrying out their mother's request? It seems that they did. Interpreting words correctly and storing them in our minds gives us an advantage over those who are careless in such matters. On more occasions than I want to remember, I failed because I didn't listen carefully to the instructions. The art of listening is a much-needed ministry. It is hard work, requiring patience, discipline, attentiveness, an open, prayerful, forgiving, selfless yet confident spirit. We can start with any of these areas and after improving move on to the next until our ministry on earth is finished. Surely we will never conquer them all.

Second, we read so much today about our need for independence, building self-esteem, and making it on our own that we sometimes forget the value of teamwork, cooperation, and building on someone else's work. The new word in business is networking, but it works in our religious, political, and social lives as well. When the widow told Elisha what she had left in the house he said, "It is enough." There are times when we need to question someone's instructions and then there are times we need to cooperate and just do it. Most of us know more about how to do the Lord's work than we will ever do. It has been my experience as an army chaplain, denominational worker, teacher, and trainer that often those who are so enthusiastic to attend a training event are not as eager to change their behavior and/or lifestyle in order to achieve the desired goal they are seeking after. King Whitney Jr. may have said it best when he wrote that the psychological impact on your mind just from changing what you are doing can change failure into success. "To the fearful it is threatening because that means that things may get worse. To the hopeful it is encouraging because things may get better. To the confident it is inspiring because the challenge exists to make things better" (King).

How great do you want your ministry to be? How successful do your want your Bible study class? How good can your committee or organization carry out its task? These questions challenge us to consider what size vessel we need to bring to the table. A one-quart dish cannot hold two quarts; neither can a weak spirit fill your spiritual cup full and running over. Communication, paying attention to detail, and following through on one's commitments are only small portions of what it takes to be successful. The question is how big will we build for the kingdom? How willing are you to go that extra mile? Is it okay to risk for something greater by setting a higher goal for yourself and others? Even if you do not hit your highest goal, you will achieve more than if you set a smaller goal. The widow's success began with the instructions: get as many empty vessels as you can. I wish I would remember to listen and pay more attention to the words that are spoken, don't you?

For Further Bible Study

1. Trace the life of Moses in the book of Exodus and discover how important following through with God's directions was to his success or failure.

2. What was the cause that killed the man listening to Paul preach in Acts 20:9?

3. In 1 Samuel 1, choose one sentence or action that helped Hannah's quest for a child become a reality.

For Personal Growth

1. What, in your opinion, is the difference between a person who is obsessive compulsive with details and another who gives attention to detail? Which one are you?

2. How important is teamwork in your church, Bible study class, or committee? Are there opportunities for team building and training in any of these areas? Investigate your answer and see what is available.

3. Make a list of people who have been a blessing to you in your personal and spiritual growth. Look over the list and ask yourself if you have ever told them how important they were. If not and they are still living, contact them and tell them today what their words and assistance meant to you.

Words of Friendship and Comfort

RUTH SAID TO NAOMI...

"I WILL GO WHERE YOU GO."
RUTH 1:16

RELATIONSHIPS GROW OR DIE; THEY NEVER STAY THE SAME OVER TIME.

What words do you use to build a lasting relationship with someone you really care about? It is not as easy to do as we may think. Millions of formerly married couples and friends are evidence that a lasting relationship is hard to maintain. Why is it that some people are so successful with words that will build a permanent relationship and others who seem to have a good education, abundant gifts, and language skills can't find the right words? Hollywood actors and actresses can bring audiences to tears or on their feet with applause but can't find the words to make a marriage commitment last for more than a couple of years. A politician's rhetoric can go on and on, but the words that they need to build trust between themselves and their constituents are often aggressive or phony. Using the right words is important for building relationships, but there is more to it than just the words. Who has not been taken in by someone whose actions didn't match the meaning of his or her words? I believe that it all starts with the meaning we give to the words we speak. In the cartoon *b.c.,* a woman says to the fat lady, "What was your favorite party game as a little girl?" "Spin the bat," she replies. "You mean spin the bottle!" says the other woman. "I got a lot fewer rejections when I used a bat," replied the fat lady (Hart). Using the right symbol sometimes helps clarify the rules. *b.c.*'s fat lady never minces her words, but you may not like the results or the relationship that ensues. Saying what you mean and meaning what you say could certainly improve a host of relationship problems. "You never tell me you love me anymore," the woman said to her husband. "I told you I loved you when I married you, didn't I?" he said. "Well if I ever change my mind, I'll tell you. Until then you can assume I still do." Lasting relationships need maintenance. When was the last time you intentionally did something to strengthen the bond between yourself and a friend or loved one? When will you do it again, but this time with a different tactic or deeper meaning?

Before we go too far down this road looking for answers, how important are relationships to having a fruitful, successful life? A Harvard Business School professor wrote an open letter to the nation's graduates telling them that in one sense they needed to forget what they had learned in school. He said that schools tend to put too much emphasis on the idea that success comes as a result of passing tests. He also said that too much emphasis is put on individual performance rather than on a group's effort and cooperation. In real life, he pointed out, doing well in the workplace and in a personal relationship depends largely on learning how to succeed in our everyday relationships (*Our Daily Bread*, 1986). My view is a little different. A relationship is not a strategy or a learned skill that comes from years of refining one's understanding of group behavior. A relationship begins with two people who care deeply about meeting the other's needs and success. A person's social class, race, religious beliefs, or economic status may limit some relationships. Former President Harry Truman said it right, "It is amazing what you can accomplish if you do not care who gets the credit" (2008). From this behavior we learn that in return for another's success we will have our own needs met. Lasting relationships are built on the success of more than one person. While any or all of these factors may hold some influence, they are not the major factors on which a relationship is built. "You can make more friends in two months by becoming interested in other people than you can in two years by trying to get other people interested in you" (Carnegie, 2007). The words that count in relationships are empathy, compassion, care, dependability, trust, understanding, and love. These behaviors are at the heart of our Christian faith. Without these, our behaviors make language and communication skills only another human voice, not someone who is unique or different. Why should anyone choose the Christian life if it is not a better life from the one they now have without Christ?

Relationships are built and structured around many different characteristics and form out of a variety of circumstances. David and Jonathan had a close personal relationship. Esther and Mordecai had a relationship created out of an ethnic crisis. Solomon and the Queen of Sheba, as heads of state, had a social/political relationship. Nehemiah built his leader/follower relationship with the exiles along the way from Babylon to Jerusalem and then in the work that followed after his arrival. Why couldn't Saul and David or Nabal and Abigail have one? David seemed willing. Saul was threatened and viewed David as a rival for his kingdom. Nabal was egotistical and self-centered and seemed to care little about his relationship with Abigail. Is a relationship built by doing something together? Sometimes it is, but not always. There was a vast difference between the lifestyles of Eli and young Samuel, but they had a relationship. You see relationships are not hard to define if you know what to look for. It has been the thesis of this book from the beginning that our words and actions make a difference in the lives of people we meet, work, and live with. Proof can easily be found if you know where to look and listen for it. A group of seminary students made a trip to a university laboratory where a specialist in neurology gave them a lecture on the brain. He showed them a laboratory brain specimen. The neurologist spoke about how the brain is nourished and stimulated by positive meaningful relationships with people. When there is an absence of this, he suggested, the brain suffers. Human beings need to know the facts about adequate brain stimulation to form meaningful and enriching relationships. One might expect to hear such things in a sermon, but not from a neurologist in a pathology lab (Oates). It seems obvious then that while brain damage may come from injury, inadequate oxygen supply, or a vitamin deficiency, one way to strengthen the neurological pathways in the brain is to develop quality relationships with people.

In Ruth and Naomi's story we find words and actions that built a lasting relationship. Naomi lived in a troubled time under difficult circumstances. Some may view her circumstances as the reason for her negative attitude. Her husband died first, then her two sons, which left her without financial support. Her future looked bleak with little hope for some quality of life. Maybe it was a combination of events that made her a little negative about her future. We read that, when Ruth and Naomi returned to Bethlehem from Moab, a woman asked, "Is this Naomi?" And Naomi responded, "Don't call me Naomi, call me Mara, for the Almighty has dealt very bitterly with me. I went out full, but the Lord has brought me back empty" (Ruth 1:19–20, nasb). Under such conditions it is not unusual for a person to become bitter, depressed, or both. But Naomi had a daughter-in-law named Ruth who made a difference. Ruth started with a simple daughter/mother-in law relationship and built an enduring bond between them that lasted throughout the remainder of their lives together.

Back in Bible days when a woman's husband died, unless she was well off financially or someone took her into their own family, she often lived in poverty for the rest of her life. Naomi returned to Bethlehem, her birthplace, with the hope of finding someone who could care for her and provide security for her in her old age. When her two sons died, both daughters-in-law started out by providing comfort and support. Naomi thanked them for their compassion and care, but indicated that they did not need to return with her to Bethlehem. Orpah, at Naomi's request, left and went back to Moab. Ruth however clung to Naomi saying,

> ...do not urge me to leave you or turn back from following you; for where you go, I will go, and where you lodge, I will lodge. Your people shall be my people, and your God, my God. And where you die, I will die, and there I will be buried. Thus may the Lord do to me, and worse, if anything but death parts you and me.
>
> Ruth 1:15–17, NASB

Naomi gave in and allowed Ruth to go with her to Bethlehem in time for the barley harvest. Together they traveled back to Bethlehem. They must have talked about a brighter future and a better life. Many questions must have passed through Naomi and Ruth's minds on that road from Moab to Bethlehem. Would they find sustenance and a place to live? Would Ruth's compassion for Naomi prove to be a blessing or another dark spot in Naomi's struggle to survive? Ruth was not Jewish. Would she, coming from Moab, be accepted in Israel? If Ruth and Naomi couldn't make it together with the help of a kinsman, would one or both have to turn to prostitution to live? Women are generally more vulnerable than men when hard times come. Fortunately there were no children to care for. What most of us want in life is certainty, the ability to predict what our lives will be like tomorrow and the next day, the next week, and in the years to come. But there never is any guarantee that we will find certainty with enough assurance that we can know without a doubt that the road we choose will bring us blessings, joy, and happiness. Certainty cannot be guaranteed in this life whether you are rich or poor, cared for by hundreds of servants, or protected by the military. There is no assurance for happiness and a good life. Television and the movies often lead us to believe that the good life is available for everyone. And if you are not enjoying the good life it is because someone is taking it away from you. Such a belief is a mistaken notion that leads to many false conclusions and potential trauma. While each of us may be able to describe what the good life is in some detail, we soon realize that our definition seldom comes close to resembling someone else's good life definition. Both of these women had experienced tragedy and loss. Ruth lost a husband. Naomi lost a husband and two sons. Could these two form a relationship that would be even close to an agreed definition of a good life?

Ruth's compassion and support for Naomi began as soon as the two of them arrived in Bethlehem. Ruth started to look for work. She was a stranger in a foreign land yet willingly put herself at risk in order to put food on their table. Ruth requested permission to go into the barley fields and glean behind the reapers picking the grains that dropped on the ground. Naomi granted her request and rapidly their relationship began to build. Soon the old daughter/mother-in-law relationship started to fade and change as Naomi and Ruth worked together to build a better future.

Now, let's look at why words are so important in building and maintaining a high quality relationship. Dr. Harold Bennett said, "Be careful in the choice of words and in your relationships with others" (*Outreach Magazine*, 1989). The wrong choice of words can ruin a great relationship in seconds. Words and actions are so hard to retrieve and take back once they are spoken and committed. A top executive placement firm president identified five points that cause most management failures: Starting with the greatest failure he identified: personality conflicts, lack of interpersonal skills, language-environmental problems, communication problems, and failure to break up problems into manageable units. Four of these five points have to do with getting along and communicating with the people you work with (*Proclaim Magazine,* 1991).

Ruth had compassion for Naomi's suffering. Ruth lost her husband also. But from the beginning she was determined not to leave Naomi destitute and alone to fend for herself. Ruth realized that as the younger of the two, she had a better chance to marry or find work that would support them both. Her compassion was found in her actions as well as in her words. James says in his epistle, chapter 2, verse 18, "show me your faith without the works, and I will show you my faith by my works" (nasb). Ruth's words expressed her compassion. Her works proved it. Doing the right thing always starts us in the right direction. Dr. Laura, in her book *How Could You Do That,* emphasizes what she calls the three C's: character, courage, and conscience. The book begins with this statement: "The path to solid, supportive, healthy relationships, self-respect, and a quality of life starts with the usually painful decision to do the right thing" (1998). I can agree with General Norman Schwarzkopf who said, "The truth of the matter is that you always know the right thing to do. The hard part is doing it" (*To Inspire Newsletter,* 2002). Think about it. Has doing the right thing always been easy for you? It surely hasn't for me and I have made some pretty foolish mistakes because I was careless, fudged, and didn't tell all I should have or didn't speak up when I knew something was wrong.

We are taught as children to say the right things at the right time. Most of us learned the words to say, but some of us missed a lot of the meaning that was supposed to go with those words. For example, a man says, "I am so sorry that you lost your husband. If there is anything I can do just call me." It sounds good. Most of us have said these exact words or ones very similar. But many of us never followed them up with good works. Our compassion was words without action even though we may have had good intentions. Our words never supported our relationship. Sometimes our words make the relationship worse. In defense some will say, "I expected her to call; if she didn't it isn't my fault…I meant what I said." Yes, you did, but the brokenhearted in their crisis often hear lots of kind words, but do not take them seriously to mean what they say. Ruth followed up her words, "I will go where you go," by going. Ruth went into the fields to glean barley because her words, "Where you live I will live," didn't put food on the table until someone went to work. Building a relationship is not just words. It is about the right words with the right meaning followed up by some action. Right words and right actions build relationships. If either is missing the relationship will decline and die. Many relationships are already dead from a failure to understand the importance of these two ideas. Some relationships will never mend because revenge, immaturity, lustful desires, resistance, indecision, ignorance, blindness, and emotional or sinful behaviors led each party down a different path. In most cases one or both parties are unwilling to recognize or accept that the relationship is dead. I received a humorous e-mail some time back that told about how relationships are broken by misunderstanding the spoken word. A couple had been debating buying a vehicle for weeks. He wanted a truck. She wanted a fast little sports-like car so she could zip through traffic around town. He would probably have settled on any beat up old truck, but everything she seemed to like was way out of their price range. "Look!" she said. "I want something that goes from 0 to 200 in just a few seconds. Nothing else will do. My birthday is coming up so surprise me!" He did just that. For her birthday, he bought her a brand new bathroom scale. Nobody has seen or heard from him since (Chesborough, 2005). I don't think they were in agreement about the final product.

As a counselor, I seldom have to dig very deep with people who are in broken relationships to discover that words and actions are the reasons behind a relationship's failure. For most of us, our formal education does not include courses in communication, problem solving, or crisis intervention. We learn most of those skills from experience after the fact. The book of Ruth is a marvelous, loving story about building relationships as you go. At the beginning of the book is a wonderful story of compassion and care that brought Ruth from Moab to Bethlehem where she intended to care for Naomi. Sometimes readers miss this first story seeing only the love story where Boaz married Ruth. Ruth's words, if said often with tenderness and followed with compassion and action, could save a lot of daughter/mother-in-law relationships. What woman, man, or friend would ever be disappointed with words and actions that said simply, "I'll go with you, and when hard times come I will be there for you"? We express similar statements in our marriage vows. May I recommend that you give these words a try and see if they don't make a difference? Relationships grow or die; they never stay the same over time. The right words and actions can cement a relationship for life. But we need to keep finding new ways to say and prove that we care. Think about it! What you say and how you act does make a difference.

For Further Bible Study

1. Who, in your opinion, was the better friend to someone in need?
   a. Barnabas for taking John Mark on a missionary journey when Paul wouldn't take him? Acts 15:39
   b. Aquilla and Priscilla who took Apollos and

instructed him in the way of God more accurately? Acts 18:26

2. Naomi's grief is understandable. How did David receive the news and handle his grief after the death of his two sons? See 2 Samuel 12:15–23 and 2 Samuel 18:32–33.

3. How excited was Ananias to befriend Paul after the Damascus road conversion in Acts 9:10?

For Personal Growth

1. Think about one or two of the best or worst relationships in your experience. What were the reasons for their success or failure?

2. In a previous chapter there is the illustration of the soul winner standing outside the adult video store trying to save one soul. Was his concern and compassion justified in your opinion even if no one accepted his help? Why?

3. Pick a current crisis in your city, state, or nation and pose this question: "Would showing compassion and working together build a satisfactory solution, or would it increase the tension and strife?"

JONATHAN SAID TO DAVID...

"WE HAVE SWORN FRIENDSHIP."

1 SAMUEL 20:42

FRIENDS MAKE LIFE EXCITING AND WORTH-WHILE.

Think with me back to your childhood days. Somewhere in your home there is probably a picture of you and your best friend…arms around each other's shoulders…looking at the camera…friends forever. Remember when you said to your friend in a soft voice, "Swear you won't tell anyone about this!" There were some things that you could only tell someone you really trusted. Then you grew older, times changed and you made other friends with whom you shared those most intimate life experiences. Time does change things; now at my age I do not have to swear most my friends, who also are around seventy years old, to secrecy because after a few hours or days most of us cannot remember what the secret was anymore anyway.

> There is an old story about two childhood friends who met again after many years. One said to the other, "You were always so organized in school, did you manage your life well?" "Yes," said her friend. "My first marriage was to a millionaire; my second marriage was to an actor; my third marriage was to a preacher; and now I'm married to an undertaker." Her friend asked, "What do those marriages have to do with a well planned life?" "Well," replied the friend, "It was one for the money, two for the show, three to get ready, and four to go."
>
> Preston Dye
> *Farmer's Almanac*

Where are those high school friends today? Some have gone on to be with the Lord…some moved away and you lost contact with them…some still live in your old neighborhood and you still call or visit, and some have been your friends for life no matter where you lived or when they moved away. Jonathan and David were not children, but grown men who took an oath to have a friendship for life. Their words went deeper than just a childhood secret and a promise not to tell their parents. Their oath came about because of an unusual set of circumstances. Jonathan's father was Saul, King of Israel, who hated David for two reasons. First, he probably knew that Samuel, at God's command, had anointed David as his replacement. Second, he hated David because he was so popular with the people after he slew Goliath. Saul's fears were not totally unfounded. The people did love David because of his victories over Israel's enemies. Saul tried unsuccessfully to kill David on several occasions. Each time David escaped. When David and Jonathan made their covenant for life, David was in hiding because it was Saul's intention to kill him. Carefully the two young men worked out a secret time and place to meet. Knowing that this friendship would be a problem for both of them, they departed swearing to maintain their friendship forever, no matter what circumstances came up against them. Jonathan said, "Go in peace, for we have sworn friendship with each other in the name of the Lord, saying, 'The LORD is witness between you and me, and between your descendants and my descendants forever'" (1 Samuel 20:42, nasb). Then Saul discovered their friendship. His anger burned against Jonathan, and he said to him, "You son of a perverse, rebellious woman! Do I not know that you are choosing the son of Jesse to your own shame and to the shame of your mother's nakedness?" (1 Samuel 20:30, nasb).

In a spiritual bond there is a relationship that goes beyond being just a friend. "Good friends are hard to find, harder to leave, and impossible to forget" (Franklin, 2001). However, I think we often use the word *friend* when we are really talking about someone who is just an acquaintance. An acquaintance is some-one you know, but not necessarily someone with whom you choose to share life's deep intimate moments and truths. With an acquaintance you carry on a conversa-tion, maybe even attend some events together, or help one another out with some difficult situation. But there is no spiritual bond between the two of you. The word *acquaintance* may sound awkward because it is not a commonly used word, but it does describe reality for most of our day-to-day relationships. Social psycholo-gists use an archery target as a way of explaining rela-tionships. Those in the outer rings are those we know the least about. As we move closer to the center of the target, we move toward those with whom we have the closest relationships. If you were to list people in this manner, you may find that there are people in the cen-ter who are closer to you than family members who are on the outer rings further away from the center. On Jonathan's target, his father Saul may have been on one of those outer rings while David rested closer toward the center. It is my belief that friends are different from acquaintances.

Think about this. In a two hundred-member church probably around 50% seldom or never attend. So you may really have eighty or ninety acquaintances and only ten to twenty friends. Some acquaintances you hardly know at all. You may serve on a committee with four or five people, but they are not necessarily friends. Occasionally you may go out to eat together or fellowship over a meal with people you have known for years, but do you have a spiritual bond with them. Would they defend you from enemies, protect you with their life if needed, and guard your most treasured secrets? Most people we know do not meet that high a standard. Sharing worship brings us together in the family of God, but it does not mean we have a spiritual bond that ties us in life or death situations. In most churches, the folks we know fall into a group we should really call "our acquaintances" because that is all they really are. We know each other's name or can recognize each other at a distance, but not as our spiritual brothers and sisters in Christ. Is it not true that as Christians we sometimes gather for worship with people with whom we are angry or care little about? There may even be some we wish we didn't have to worship with at all, yet we all claim to be a part of God's family. On Sunday, we gather with some with whom we have no spiritual bond or friendship at all. Jonathan and David had a spiritual bond that went beyond sharing a common worship experience. Developing a spiritual bond with another believer is difficult. It requires a covenant of commitment and trust that reaches deep into our own identity. Jesus said in John 15:13, "Greater love has no one than this, that one lay down his life for his friends" (nasb). Most Christians are not willing to make this kind of commitment. The poet Emerson said, "The glory of friendship is not the outstretched hand, nor the kindly smile nor the joy of companionship; it is the spiritual inspiration that comes to one when he discovers that someone else believes in him and is willing to trust him" (2008). That is what it means to spiritually bond with another human being. Because David and Jonathan had such a spiritual bond, they also had an abiding trust in each other and a commitment to protect that relationship whatever the cost. It is reasonable to assume that not everyone you know or have an association with will be your spiritual partner. When we are spiritually bonded with someone, we are more than just friends…we truly become brothers and sisters in the Lord. Priscilla and Aquilla had it, Paul and Timothy had it, and so did Jonathan and David.

Sometimes our relationship with people is not as strong as it should be. As a result there may be a time when some event or activity calls for a third party to serve as a witness. It is not unusual in these situations for a reference to be made asking the Lord to be a witness between two people who seek a deeper relationship. Often marriage vows or legal papers ask for God to serve as a witness to newly established covenants and contracts. Notice that the words spoken here resemble another covenant found in scripture. See if you agree with me. Laban said to Jacob, "May the LORD keep watch between you and me when we are away from each other" (Genesis 31:49, nasb). This covenant between Laban and Jacob was also a covenant for protection and security. But these words were not given to establish a spiritual bond between friends. While Jonathan and

David were friends, Laban and Jacob were not. Both called on the Lord to be a witness to their covenant saying they acknowledged the Lord's presence at this moment in time. Laban and Jacob swore their covenant in the open among family and never saw each other again. David and Jonathan met in secret to create a covenant that extended beyond their present crisis with Saul. David rekindled this bond with Jonathan's son, Mephibosheth, long after Saul and Jonathan were killed in a war with the Philistines. For protection as well as a public oath, we call on the Lord to be a witness for us in situations where there is a need for a covenant to protect or secure the relationship between friends or enemies. An oath taken in the name of the Lord in a court of law or a marriage vow is supposed to be sincere and truthful. Who among us has not given sworn testimony in a court of law or pledged their solemn vow in marriage using the phrase…"So help me God"? But may I submit to you that some oaths or vows are simply words that are hurriedly spoken, like those uttered by Peter around the fire in the high priest's court, without thinking about the consequences. Even though we call on the Lord as our witness, if our words are not honest or truthful, but spoken in haste to get us through some present moment or difficulty, would we still want the Lord to be our witness?

Len Broughton tells the story of an old judge in the Georgia mountains who knew little about the law, but had a strong commitment to it. One day a witness was seated in the witness chair covered with a shawl around him. The judge said, "You're here to bear testimony?" "Yes," said the witness. "Put up your right hand," "It is paralyzed." "Hold up your left then." "The left arm is off." "Stick up your foot." "Both of them got shot off in the late war." "Then stand on your head. You have got to put up something in this court to show you mean what you say."

(Unknown)

In a court of law, our words become a witness against us if we falsely testify that what we say is the truth when it is not. Many situations demand that we have a witness who certifies that an oath was taken. Perjury is a serious offense. How many of us would be convicted of perjury for things we have said to our friends and family if the truth were really known? When my wife asks me if the new piece of furniture she purchased goes well with the other pieces of furniture in our home, I am not going to tell her a lie, but I may not tell her all that I am thinking either. There is no sense in making more problems by lying. Jacob in Genesis 31:53 does not swear by his God, but by the "fear of his father Isaac" (nasb). Jacob had been such a thief and conniver that these words may have been the best he could say for he had not yet had his spiritual renewal and commitment experience with the Lord at Bethel. A spiritual commitment calls for a witness who knows the truth and understands this to be a sacred oath. Jesus, in the Sermon on the Mount, taught us something new and different about oaths when he said,

> ...do not swear at all: either by heaven, for it is God's throne; or by the earth, for it is his footstool; or by Jerusalem, for it is the city of the Great King. And do not swear by your head, for you cannot make even one hair white or black. Simply let your 'Yes' be 'Yes,' and your 'No,' 'No'; anything beyond this comes from the evil one.
>
> Matthew 5:34, (NASB)

Clyde Tilley, in his excellent commentary on Jesus' teaching in the Sermon on the Mount says, "...the point is Jesus' requirement of complete integrity and total honesty would make oaths unnecessary" (Tilley, 1992). So was Jonathan and David's covenant with God as a witness necessary? Yes, it was! In Jonathan and David's day, such an expression meant that they trusted that the Lord would help them carry out their words. Do we mean the same thing today when we say, "Lord help us" or "as God is my witness"? For most of us, these are just words and expressions that we use in hoping others will believe what we are saying. Today's moral relativism says that whether your answer is true or false depends on the circumstances and situation. We have come to the place where we believe lying is okay. Friends do not lie to one another, neither do they need the Lord as a third party to witness their commitment. If we have the Holy Spirit in our hearts, we have all the witness we will ever need. Our spiritual bond will carry us through the difficult moment. David could get through the difficulty with Saul because he had a covenant with Jonathan. A spiritual bond in one relationship can often help us through another problem with someone else.

Friendships can and should extend to our families. Sometimes even our friend's friend or a friend's family member becomes our friend too. Many years later David recalled this moment when he and Jonathan pledged their friendship in a covenant before the Lord. In 2 Samuel 9 we can read about David's remembrance of his covenant with Jonathan.

> The king asked, "Is there no one still left of the house of Saul to whom I can show God's kindness?" Ziba answered the king, "There is still a son of Jonathan; he is crippled in both feet." "Where is he?" the king asked. Ziba answered, "He is at the house of Makir son of Ammiel in Lo-debar." So King David had him brought from Lo-debar, from the house of Makir son of Ammiel. When Mephibosheth son of Jonathan, the son of Saul, came to David, he bowed down to pay him honor. David said, "Mephibosheth." And he said, "Here is your servant!" David said to him, "Do not fear, for

I will surely show kindness to you for the sake of
your father Jonathan and I will restore to you all
the land that belonged to your grandfather Saul and
you shall eat at my table regularly."

2 Samuel 9:3–7 (NASB)

When we love a friend, sometimes we learn to love
their family as our own. That is why they are friends and
not acquaintances. Our friendship sometimes extends
to those whom our friends also love. Most of us have
at least one story about someone who had a friend and
that deep friendship extended to their friend's family. I
do not know if love extends to every college family or
not. A college president said to the coach, "Our alumni
and I love the way our team is winning games this season." "Would you love me as much if I didn't win any
games?" asked the coach. "Yes!" said the president, "but
I'd miss having you around." In some cases love is con-
ditional. When there is a spiritual bond the covenant
goes beyond who wins and who loses. David and Saul
never had that kind of friendship though he married
Michael, Saul's daughter.

Even if friendships have closure and end, the covenant can still remain in effect. When time and distance
separate us from friends, for a variety of reasons, we still
can have that spiritual bond. On other occasions we
outgrow our friends because we marry and/or develop
different interests. Hopefully, the reason for this change
in our friendship is only situational and not because of

anger or disappointment. Then months or years later a covenant may be reconsidered. This time it may or may not be stronger than before. If there was a spiritual bond the first time, chances are good that the covenant will be renewed. If it is not, it reminds me of the story about a person who helped a friend and was then repaid with an envelope containing a note and five used lottery tickets. The note said, "Thank you very much for your help. As a gift I bought you some lottery tickets, sorry you didn't win." How is that for friendship?

The last time Jonathan and David met is found in 1 Samuel 23:18. "The two of them made a covenant before the LORD. Then Jonathan went home, but David remained at Horesh" (nasb). This situation brought closure to their friendship. Both knew the costs and difficulties that went with their friendship. Saul's anger kept David in hiding until he had to join the Philistines, Saul's enemies, to escape death at Saul's hand. David was no lover of the Philistines. They used the division between David and Saul to their own advantage. But it was a safe place for David until Saul and Jonathan's deaths. When David went over to the Philistines, it became impossible for him to meet with Jonathan again. Seldom do we have a successful closure to friendships when we are found in rival armies fighting over the same territory or property.

A friend shared this story with me. I have read or heard it before, but do not know the source.

On a cold day in 1942, inside a Nazi concentration

camp, a lone, young boy looks beyond the barbed wire and sees a young girl pass by. She too is moved by his presence. In an effort to give expression to her feelings, she throws a red apple over the fence—a sign of life, hope, and love. The young boy bends over, picks up the apple. A ray of light has pierced his darkness. The following day, thinking he is crazy for even entertaining the notion of seeing this young girl again, he looks out beyond the fence, hoping. On the other side of the barbed wire, the young girl yearns to see again this tragic figure that moved her so. She comes prepared with apple in hand. Despite another day of wintry blizzards and chilling air, two hearts are warmed once again as the apple passes over the barbed wire. The scene is repeated for several days. The two young spirits on opposite sides of the fence look forward to seeing each other, if only for a moment and if only to exchange a few words. The interaction is always accompanied by an exchange of inexplicably heartening feelings. At the last of these momentary meetings, the young boy greets his sweet friend with a frown and says, "Tomorrow, don't bring me an apple, I will not be here. They are sending me to another camp." The young boy walks away, too heartbroken to look back. From that day forward the calming image of the sweet girl would appear to him in moments of anguish. Her eyes, her words, her thoughtfulness, her red apple, all were a recurring vision that would break his nighttime sweats. His family died in the war. The life he had known had all but vanished, but this one memory remained alive and gave him hope. In 1957 in the United States, two adults, both immigrants, are set up on a blind date. "And where were you during the war?" inquires the woman. "I was in a concentration camp in Germany," the man replies. "I remember I used to throw apples over the fence to a boy who was in a concentration camp," she recalls. With a feeling of shock, the man speaks. "And did that boy say to you one day, "Don't bring an apple anymore because I am being sent to another camp?" "Why, yes," she responds, "but how could you possibly know that?" He looks into her eyes and says, "I was that young boy." There is a brief silence, and then he continues, "I was separated from you then, and I don't ever want to be without you again. Will you marry me?" They embrace one another as she says, "Yes." On Valentine's Day 1996, on national telecast of the Oprah Winfrey show, this same man affirmed his enduring love to his wife of 40 years. "You fed me in the concentration camp," he said. "You fed me throughout all these years; now, I remain hungry if only for your love." The darkest moments of one's life may carry the seeds for the brightest tomorrow. Never give up hope.

Priddy 03/9/99

Not all friendships find such closure. Jonathan and David's friendship ended that day in Horesh. It was not revived again until many years later when David asked the question of Ziba, "Is there yet anyone left of the house of Saul, that I may show him kindness for Jonathan's sake?" (2 Samuel 9:3 nasb) Maybe it is time we ask ourselves: what ever happened to my friend in high school or college? Maybe it is time to find out. Perhaps we can renew an old friendship. Perhaps we can do something for their children or a family member as David did. Is it time to recall that day when we swore our friendship and go from there as the Lord leads? Maybe it is time to think those words that established the covenant that spiritually bonded us to another person in God's kingdom.

For Further Bible Study

1. Paul and a young companion were on a mission trip and the young man left and went home. Later Paul considers his friendship and presence important and sends for him to come to Rome where he is in jail. Who was the young man?

2. How important is a friend? What does Jesus say in John 15:13?

3. Friends are not always wise, nor should their advice always be taken. Study 2 Samuel 13 and find out how Absalom's friend led him into difficulty.

For Personal Growth

1. Choose two people you know. Put each name at the top of a piece of paper. Draw a line down the middle of each page. Title one column "characteristics and behaviors I like." Title the other column "characteristics I do not like." Now list as many things as you can for things you like or don't like about each person in the appropriate column. When you finish, the list should tell you why one is a friend and the other is only an acquaintance.

2. When you make a covenant or agreement with a friend, what makes you feel you need to keep it? Make a list and see. What does your list tell you about your relationship?

3. Take a couple of days' newspapers and search for articles where friends have participated in some activity together. What mutual benefit or hazards came from their relationship?

ABIGAIL SAID TO DAVID…

"ON ME ALONE, MY LORD, BE THE BLAME."

1 SAMUEL 25:24

THE WISE KNOW WHAT TO SAY AND WHEN TO SAY IT.

When was the last time someone you knew took the blame for something wrong that happened to you? For most of us it is against our nature to admit we are wrong, at least that is what my wife says about me. Like most husbands I do not want to be reminded of my mistakes. Hopefully it doesn't go as far as this classic illustration. A new pastor asked a Sunday school class, "Who broke down the walls of Jericho?" No one answered. Finally a boy said, "Not me, sir!" Upset, the pastor asked the teacher, "Is this typical?" She said, "I believe this boy is honest and I really don't think he did it." The pastor went to the head deacon. "I've known the boy and the teacher for years," he said, "and neither of them would do such a thing." Aghast, the pastor went to the chairman of the Christian education board with the problem, and he suggested that they just pay for the damage and charge it off to maintenance (*Our Daily Bread*, 1991). Finding out who is to blame is a big adventure today. Take a few minutes to listen or study the media, local, state, or national politicians and you will find that they are always pushing for an investigation into finding out why something happened and who is to blame. And just like me, seldom will any politician admit his or her mistakes until they are forced to.

Abigail's husband, Nabal, was in his field in Maon near Carmel when David sent ten young men to go up to greet him and find out if he would provide food to feed David's army. David's men did as they were asked and greeted Nabal saying, "Have a long life, peace be to you and peace be to your house and peace be to all that you have" (1 Samuel 25:6, nasb). They then shared with him how they had not robbed his sheepfold nor abused his men and asked him to "…share whatever you find at hand to your servants and to your son David." Nabal responded, "Who is David? And who is the son of Jesse?…Shall I then take my bread and water and my meat that I have slaughtered for my shearers, and give it to men whose origin I do not know?" (1 Samuel 25:2–12, nasb).

David's men left bewildered, returning to David telling him what Nabal said. David was livid and immediately told his men to gird themselves with their swords. He divided his men, leaving some with the baggage while the others followed him to Nabal's house. About the same time after David's men left Nabal's property to return back to David, one of Nabal's servants returned to the house and spoke to Abigail, Nabal's wife. He told her how Nabal had scorned David's men. Abigail quickly took 200 loaves of bread and two jugs of wine and five sheep already prepared plus five measures of roasted grain and 100 clusters of raisins and 200 cakes of figs and loaded them on donkeys and set out toward David's camp. When she met him on the way to her house, she dismounted, fell at his feet, and said,

> On me alone, my lord, be the blame. And please let your maidservant speak to you and listen to the words of your maidservant. Please do not let my lord pay attention to this worthless man, Nabal for as his name is so is he. Nabal is his name and folly is with him; but I your maidservant did not see the young men of my lord whom you sent...And now let this gift which your maidservant brought to my lord be given to the young men who accompany my lord. Please forgive the transgression of your maidservant...because my lord is fighting the battles of the Lord and evil shall not be found in you all your days.
>
> 1 Samuel 25:28 (NASB)

Abigail's words and quick action saved Nabal's life. David replied, "...blessed be your discernment and blessed be you who have kept me this day from bloodshed, and from avenging myself by my own hand" (1 Samuel 15:33, nasb). Abigail's quick response with foodstuffs for David's men and accepting the blame for Nabal's verbal abuse saved his life. Her failure to get involved could have been immediate death for her husband and maybe the loss of all his wealth and material goods at David's hand. Most of us know a few men or women who fit Nabal's mold. They are rude, unmannered, and coarse in their conversation and impersonal in public relationships. And to make matters worse, they either don't care about how they are perceived or they fail to learn from their mistakes. Wealth may have bought Nabal friends, but not so for David, who came within a hair of making the ground equal between those who have wealth and those who have the power of the sword to take away another man's wealth.

Verse 33 in the King James Version translates David's interpretation of Abigail's apology as "advice," while the New American Standard Bible uses "discernment" (1 Samuel 25:33–39). I like the latter word because it signifies to me the ability to know and understand the levels that go with public discourse and conversations. The word in Hebrew is tah'-am, which has a variety of meanings: a taste, figurative perception; advice, behavior, decree, discretion, intelligence, judgment, reason, taste, or understanding (Strong, 1850).

No matter which version you choose, it is Abigail's wisdom to understand when her husband has carelessly gotten himself and his family into trouble with David and his men. She blames herself and asks forgiveness for her foolish husband. Abigail requests forgiveness resulting in David softening his anger and his returning to the camp after accepting her gifts. When Abigail returns from her meeting with David, Nabal is having a drunken party. She says nothing until the next day and tells him what she has done. Scripture says his heart "died within him and he became as a stone" (1 Samuel 25:37, nasb). When David heard that Nabal was dead, David sent a proposal to Abigail to become his wife, and she accepted.

This passage presents us with a few important questions. For example, why was David willing to spare Nabal after Abigail's apology when he had so little compassion with others who turned against him? Why did the Lord spare Nabal for tens days and then bring his life to an end? Why was David so quick to take Abigail as his wife immediately after Nabal's death when he already had several wives? I think the answer to all these questions is that the Lord honors forgiveness and repentance no matter when or where it happens. Abigail's words represent the spirit that scripture teaches. The point is not Nabal's ten-day extension, David's marriage to Abigail, or his military prowess, but the power of words to change the human heart from revenge to a grant of forgiveness and peace.

Societies, families, and individuals need to be reminded often that when forgiveness is genuinely requested, unless there is evidence to the contrary, it should be granted. If forgiveness does not happen, then change cannot occur. Why ask for forgiveness if either party does not desire to restore the relationship? Why search your heart and ask God's spirit to convict you of your transgression if there is no hope that forgiveness will granted? In the Lord's Prayer we have the answer. We are to ask whether the other person in the relationship desires it or not. We ask so our Heavenly Father can forgive our sins.

Abigail was in a very difficult situation. Her husband was crass, rude, and belligerent. When she heard that he had another outburst and this time against David's men, she realized only a quick response would spare her husband, family, and servants. From this passage we understand that David's request for food was not unreasonable, nor would it have robbed Nabal's family and servants of what they needed to sustain their life. Apparently Abigail's donkeys loaded with food didn't make a dent in Nabal's grocery stock, for scripture tells us he had a feast for his servants and friends while she was on the road trying to save his life. A day later, when she does tell him what she has done for him, he realizes his mistake and "his heart died within him."

Maybe Nabal's situation was not as it seems. It could be that Nabal supported Saul and didn't want to anger him by feeding David's men. Or did he think he knew something about David's character or behavior that would allow him to believe he could get away with his insulting treatment of David's men? My own opinion is that while it is an interesting question, these are not real reasons for his behavior. Why? Because we still see men and women today who live without conscience and moral values exhibiting similar excuses for their attitudes and behaviors. His outburst was uncalled for then and it would be uncalled for today. Saddam Hussein's antics in the Iraqi courtroom and Venezuelan President Hugo Chavez's outbursts in the United Nations are only a couple of modern day examples when foolish men intentionally open their mouths and spew out hate and venom as Nabal did. William Henry once said, "Fools live to regret their words, wise men to regret their silence" (*Chicago Tribune*). Words carefully chosen lead those who oppose your own views to reconsider their own understanding concerning what are the facts and needs in a situation. When we seek to enlighten others concerning their thoughts and actions, we create an environment for compromise and bipartisan support. The power of words can mean life or death depending on who says them and the timing or circumstances surrounding their speech. Jesus' words to the Jewish leaders that whoever was without sin should cast the first stone at the woman caught in adultery in John 8 is a good example. Her accusers absented themselves one by one until they were all gone. Jesus then asked the woman, "Where are your accusers, has no man condemned you?" Her repentance is found in her response, "No man, Lord." Then Jesus offered her forgiveness with a word of caution, "Neither do I condemn you; go and sin no more" (John 8:11, nasb). Angry words brought her to Jesus, and well-chosen words sent her accusers away. Likewise, Abigail's heart found peace when David turned away his wrath by her kind words and quick intervention. Introverts have an advantage in that they tend to think before they speak while extraverts tend to speak first and think later.

Look again at the anger, hatred, and slander in Nabal's words. "Who is David? And who is the son of Jesse? There are many servants today who are each breaking away from his master. Shall I then take my bread and water and my meat that I have slaughtered for my shearers, and give it to men whose origin I do not know?" (1 Samuel 25:10–11, nasb). What did Nabal hope to gain by such a vehement attack? Was it because David was not present that he felt he could get away with such an attack? Or did he just not care what words he uttered or who heard them? Nabal is not the first man to die because he uttered such hatred and slanderous speech. There have been hundreds, if not thousands, who followed down that same road to their deaths. Look at David's final words to Solomon in 1 Kings 2 for a list of people who scorned and maligned David during his lifetime and what he had Solomon do to them for their words. Jesus in Matthew 12 speaks about idle words: "…every careless word that men shall speak, they shall render account for it in the Day of Judgment. For by your words you shall be justified and by your words you shall be condemned" (Matthew 12:36–37, nasb). Solomon's wisdom tells us, "…a soft answer turns away wrath" (Proverbs 5:1, nasb). Abigail's response was quick, focused, and exactly what the situation called for. Her swift decision to load donkeys with food for David and his men gave David a different impression of Nabal's house. David's first impression of Nabal's words merited judgment and retribution. Abigail's soft words and quick response gave David an opportunity to respond with less destructive and violent actions. Why use words to push people into a fight? Why attack another person's character with hateful rhetoric when such words will stand against us when we stand in a court of law or before the Father at our judgment? Could it be because people's hearts are deceitfully wicked and from them "…can come no good thing" (Romans 7:18, kjv)?

Those reading this chapter will readily admit that most of us have learned the dangers and heartache that go with Nabal's scandalous words. Yes, words are powerful and they can determine who lives and who dies. Words provide opportunities to cool the flames of heated rhetoric before violence destroys a relationship. James, in his letter to the church, warns us that taming the tongue is difficult. His advice in chapter 3 reminds us to use caution when we speak and seek peace, sowing the fruit of righteousness (James 3:1–18, nasb).

Who are those whose words bring peace instead of the sword? Who are those whose words bring us together rather than driving us apart? It is those who use their minds to discern truth that have learned the subtleties of language and speech. For those who neither have such gifts or a willingness to learn them there is always trial and error. Christians must rise above street level words and behaviors. Our evidence to the world is that Christ in our life does make a difference in what we say and how we say it. If one is to err by making a mistake in judgment about a person's character, it should be on the side of grace, integrity, and forgiveness rather than bawdy rhetoric. There are those who have never learned how to consider another's point of view or the intricacies of a difficult situation. They only know anger as a first response. Nabal could have loaded the donkey and come to David with his apology after rethinking the situation, but he didn't. The lack of compassion or a willingness to show repentance was not in Nabal's character or lifestyle. Instead, Jesus said, "If you forgive men for their transgressions, your heavenly Father will also forgive you. But if you do not forgive men, then your Father will not forgive your transgressions" (Matthew 6:14–15, nasb). Nabal's servants were not warriors. They could not have stood in battle against David's men. Did Nabal's logic and reason escape him? Did he fall into an old habit that this time failed him? The final outcome tells us something went wrong with his thinking.

I had just turned twenty-four and was the pastor of my first church. Prior to my call, the church was forced to cut several huge diseased walnut trees on their property that were too close to the church. The branches left over from the trees were pushed up into a pile behind the church. After a few weeks, I was frustrated with this pile of brush and decided to get rid of this eyesore by asking the church for permission to burn the grass and weeds and cut the large limbs up for firewood. I was given permission, a chainsaw, and gasoline with a warning to be careful. On a cold frosty morning I set a small grass fire to burn out the weeds and overgrowth so I could get into the pile and cut up the limbs. The grass fire was smoking and hardly burning. It would burn a little, die, burn, and die very slowly. So I cranked up the chainsaw and started on the tree limbs. After a few minutes I turned around and saw the grass fire had moved from the moist frosty shade of the church to dry grass in the sunshine. The fire was skipping quickly over the dry grass and headed for a tool shed at the label factory next door to the church. This factory was the major employer in the community. I stopped the chain saw and ran over to the fire and began stomping on the fire with abandon. Each time I stomped on the fire it jumped out in every direction. I ran into the factory and called for the fire department. But it was too late; the grass fire engulfed the shed, which contained twenty-two solid cherry rocking chairs that the owner had finished before leaving for a vacation in Florida.

The fire department could not save the shed, the chairs, or any of his equipment and tools, but they did save the factory. Some weeks later the owner returned from vacation and this young red-faced preacher apologized for his foolishness. The owner said to me, "I am an old man and you are a young man. This loss is not covered by insurance and you would be a long time paying me back, so I am willing to forgive you." I stammered again an apology after realizing the financial loss involved. Quietly he listened and then remarked, "Next time before you ever start another fire, you tell everyone you know that you light one heck of a match." Not only did I learn a lesson on safety, I learned the power forgiveness has over the human soul. Nabal should have been standing before David asking for forgiveness instead of Abigail his wife, but it just wasn't in his mind that he should and the stress took his life.

Abigail seized the moment, asked for forgiveness, and turned away immediate death and destruction for her family and servants. Discernment helps you to know when an error has occurred. Forgiveness helps you to know how reconciliation can be accomplished. As believers we need to develop our minds and language skills to reach a world that needs to find and practice forgiveness rather than blame. Efforts to discover who is to blame should be left to the work of the Holy Spirit. Energies used toward reconciliation rather than justifying our own behavior often begin with understanding the power of forgiveness. I wish I had said I am sorry more often instead of looking for a good excuse, don't you? Instead of using anger as a first response to justify our behavior, we should learn that a soft answer can turn away someone's wrath.

For Further Bible Study

1. Blaming someone else is such an easy and natural thing to do. Which person in the following three passages demonstrates, for you, a person who used the poorest excuse to blame someone else for their own failure: Genesis 3:12, 1 Samuel 13:11, Joshua 7:20–21? Why did you choose this person?

2. Who is the woman that unleashes unbridled anger against an Old Testament prophet in 2 Kings 9:30–37 and as a result loses her life?

3. Which Old Testament patriarch told his sons to first ask for forgiveness as the way to heal a broken relationship with an Egyptian leader? Genesis 50:17

For Personal Growth

1. Who in your lifetime is someone that exhibited anger similar to Nabal's tirade against David's men? What was the result or what judgment did they receive for their behavior?

2. When was the last time you offered forgiveness to someone who wronged you? Recall how you felt and how they responded. Was it just a casual thing or did forgiveness bring you closer together?

3. It is so easy to blame someone else for your own failure. Check your newspaper this week for a news story where someone blamed someone else for his or her foolish actions. The blame game never ends, does it?

DAVID SAID TO MEPHIBOSHETH...

"I WILL SHOW KINDNESS TO YOU FOR YOUR FATHER'S SAKE."

2 SAMUEL 9:7

DON'T UNDERESTIMATE ANOTHER'S KINDNESSES.

We sometimes talk about the word *kindness* as if practicing it was something we do all the time. It's not easy to be kind. If human kindness was measured like the bell-shaped curve our professors and teachers used for grading tests, we might see clearly how difficult it is to get a perfect score all the time. Can you name more than one or two people who are kind all the time? It is difficult, isn't it? Most people you know are kind some of the time, and there are people who are seldom ever kind. That means the majority of people you know are somewhere in the middle of that bell shaped curve, kind most of the time, but not all of the time. King David is a good example. He had moments of kindness, but he certainly didn't exude kindness as a major life-long character trait. The Lord said to David, "You shall not build a house for my name because you are a man of war and have shed blood" (1 Chronicles 28:3, NASB). That sounds pretty specific to me that kindness was not David's middle name, yet in the scripture passage for this chapter, David is moved to show kindness to someone from Saul's family. Why? David asked a servant named Ziba, "Is there not yet anyone of the house of Saul on whom I may show the kindness of God?" (2 Samuel 9:3, NASB). Ziba responded with the news that Mephibosheth, one of Jonathan's sons, crippled in both feet was alive. Now here rests the information that makes this situation fit David's question concerning kindness and Saul's family. David had opportunity to take Saul's life on several occasions but withheld his hand because Saul was God's anointed. Until Saul died David felt no obligation to kill Saul or usurp his kingdom. However, it was not Saul to whom David had such great loyalty, but to Saul's son, Jonathan. Remember from a previous chapter how close David and Jonathan were bonded in their covenant? When David discovered that Jonathan had a son that was still living, he sent Ziba to bring him from the house of Machir in Lo-debar. Does David desire to rekindle the friendship he once had with Jonathan? Was he feeling guilty that he survived the war with the Philistines and Jonathan, his covenant partner, was slain? We cannot be certain for scripture doesn't answer these questions. But David, in the same paragraph, switches from naming the house of Saul to saying "for the sake of your father Jonathan" (1 Chronicles 28:5–7, NASB). In my opinion David's feelings are for Jonathan, not Saul's house. That spiritual bond that held them together had rekindled David's hunt for a survivor in Saul's house.

Scholars tell us that anyone who expresses altruism may be motivated to do so for a variety of reasons. Maybe they get a tax deduction or want to create a new image for themselves or gain some social or political advantage. Why are not all altruistic efforts examples of kindness? Because doing something for your own benefit rather than for someone else's is truer to our human nature than altruism (Pinker, 1997). I mentioned earlier that there are few people who are able to show kindness in almost all situations. One reason we find these people so very likeable is that there are so few of them. And then on some occasions we can only appreciate their kindness up to a point. Have you ever found yourself uncomfortable around someone who is overly kind? Christopher Plummer once said, "Working with Julie Andrews is like getting hit over the head with a Valentine" (*Good Stuff Magazine*, 2005). SOMETIMES UNUSUALLY KIND PEOPLE MAKE US FEEL UNEASY BECAUSE THEIR KINDNESS EXCEEDS OUR OWN AND WE FEEL A TINGE OF GUILT. BUT THESE EXPERIENCES ARE EXCEPTIONS. MOST OF US ENJOY FRIENDS WHO ARE KIND AND WHO EXPRESS a genuine altruistic spirit. Once a Christian business-man, embarrassed by his unwillingness to be a servant, decided to do something about his behavior. Instead of hurrying through his day and always neglecting to show humility and kindness, he promised the Lord today he would be different. When he picked up his ticket to catch the commuter train he was late, and in his hurry to get to the train he bumped into a little boy carrying a jigsaw puzzle and scattering it on the floor. It was either apologize and catch the train or help the boy. Remembering his promise he stopped and helped the boy. As the train pulled out, the boy looked at the man in a kind of awe and said, "Mister, are you Jesus?" (*Proclaim Magazine,* 1985). Would you have caught the train in time or helped the boy?

The boy's words are interpreted as we want them to be, because we store data differently from our experiences. No two people will view or interpret an event exactly alike. So when David said he wanted to show kindness to Saul's descendents, his motive may have been to strengthen his kingdom by causing those loyal to Saul to believe they could now trust him because of his kindness to Mephibosheth. David may have genuinely wanted to do some kind and good as he recalled his relationship with Jonathan. Would others, viewing this moment of kindness toward Mephibosheth, interpret David's invention differently? Of course, and they did. The word kindness didn't have the same meaning for Ziba as it did for David. He was not at all pleased with such a proposal. We read, "Then the king called Saul's servant Ziba, and said to him, 'All that belonged to Saul and to all his house I have given to your master's grandson'" (2 Samuel 9:9, nasb). Then he added that Ziba and his sons would cultivate the land and bring in the produce so that Saul's grandson may have food. Ziba and his sons would do the work and send the food to Mephibosheth who would regularly eat at David's table. Now Ziba had fifteen sons and twenty servants. David's kindness was certainly not good news for the Ziba clan. Mephibosheth probably viewed these events with great joy for he went from the status of a boarder in Machir's house in Lo-debar to a landowner eating his own food at David's table in Jerusalem. Color Mephibosheth's perspective about David happy. Ziba's view of David is colored an angry black or greenish envy. Ziba is the loser and sees nothing good that can come from such kindness to Mephibosheth. His loyalty to Saul earns him nothing. He has a huge household to feed and the labor he, his sons, and servants exert will not increase their own wealth, but Mephibosheth's. Kindness is understood differently, depending on what relationship you have to it and in whose favor the final numbers are counted.

Word meanings are still having lots of ambiguity for us today. Women in Afghanistan and Iraq interpret democracy differently than the senior male leaders do. Democracy for women means more opportunity and increased freedom over their own lives. For most men in these two countries, it lessens their control and authority over women's activities, careers, and lifestyles. For the followers of Saddam and the Taliban, democracy takes away a man's right to own a woman as property. Those once disenfranchised with few rights now have a say in the politics and culture of the nation. For the terrorists who blow themselves up with car bombs, democracy has provided them with an immediate entry into heaven and seventy waiting virgins. For those individuals and their families the martyrs destroyed, democracy is the high price citizens have to pay to be free and participate in their own destiny.

Ambiguity with words is also played out in the United States and the Western world in the nightly news broadcasts as commentators, editors, and journalists report and spin these events in the Middle East with their own neutral, good, or bad or interpretation. Whether life is fair or not sometimes boils down to how you interpret the words that are played out in your own life story. Who is the conservative Christian, and who is the fundamentalist or the moderate one? Do they wear this tag with pride or anger? Well that depends on their own interpretation, values, and experiences. For me there is less ambiguity when I choose to live in an open system where I am free to make choices. I am willing to accept the fact that words have different meanings. It wouldn't be simpler to live in a closed system where all words have the same meaning. A closed system does not offer me the same options as an open system does. A closed system may not be kind at all but ruthless and isolationist. A belief system is difficult to keep closed for a number of reasons. First, it is physiologically impossible for every human mind to agree on the definition and meaning for any word because words are not identically stored in the brain in the same way. In the language of computers, everything is either a 0 or a 1. In the human mind it is not so. There are always subtleties that give a slightly different meaning to the word based on different experiences. An open system makes room for kindness to one's enemies as found when applying Jesus' words to "love your enemies" (Matthew 5:44, nasb). Second, in a closed system culture moves toward stagnation because it eliminates any chance for individuality or change. We would all wear the same kind of clothing, drive the same color cars, and live in similarly designed houses until we reach ad nauseam. It was philanthropist Barbara Tober noted that sometimes "traditions are group efforts to keep the unexpected from happening" (*The Week*, 11/09/07). For some, to live in such a closed system makes dying a better option. Forcing people to agree on a word's meaning doesn't help much either because they will only agree with you as long as you hold power over them or they have something to gain by doing so. As soon as there is a change in the power structure, people return to their own interpretations or another one that better suits their own selfish purpose.

It not unreasonable to assume that the human

mind has different processes for different purposes. The challenge for us is to be aware of each and allow them to work together. W. Fields identified absorbing, retaining, reasoning, and creating as the key functions of the brain. This is Fields' outline and the comments in parenthesis are mine. He suggests:

> The absorptive function enables us to observe and to focus attention. Our mind pays more attention to the new, the unique, the tragic, or the dangerous observations more easily. The retentive function enables us to memorize and judge. (We know what kindness is when we see it by quickly comparing it with our sense of right and wrong.) We have a monopoly on the fourth until computers or electronic machines take it from us. (1) Creative people are sensitive to their surroundings. They have the ability to see things that go unnoticed by the average individual. (Creative people exhibit certain characteristics. They can practice kindness where they find opportunity.) (2) They have mental flexibility and can adjust to new developments and changing situations. (Kindness does not have to be overt, pointed, and open for everyone to see. Kindness can be mixed with other behaviors and emotions.) (3) They have independent judgment. They are moved more by solid evidence than feelings or opinions. (Kindness does not have to have a reason to be expressed openly because it is in the nature of the person not the situation.) (4) They have a toler-

ance for ambiguity. They recognize that some contradictions, complexities, and disorders cannot be resolved easily, simply, or quickly. (One who gives does not have to have someone who is worthy as the receiver. We can be kind to people who have made foolish selfish mistakes.) (5) They have the ability to abstract, to break down problems into their various components, to sense the relationships between variables. (People who are kind look for moments when they can inject words and acts of kindness that can turn an ugly situation around.) (6) They have the ability to synthesize to stack the blocks in new ways and come up with new methods and toys. (Kindness can be the mortar that holds the bricks together, the bricks themselves, or the process that brings it all together.) (7) They have a restless urge for solving problems and taking on tough situations (Fields, 1968). (While some may view these steps as complicated, my view is that they express very well how creative people successfully adapt, change, and respond to complicated situations. This is only one of many analyses about how the brain functions.)

What we must understand is that we can learn how to use our minds to build better relationships between people and nations. How we interpret any situation depends on who is involved and what the circumstances are. David's kindness to Mephibosheth depended on who one was; David, Mephibosheth, Ziba, or even the house of Machir may have had different opinions about what the purpose was for David's kindness. The house of Machir had been feeding, clothing, and hiding Mephibosheth for years maybe with some support from friends of Saul. Were they glad not to have the handicapped Mephibosheth as a responsibility any longer? Were they fearful that David might finally destroy the house of Saul? Scripture doesn't say. Before the final decision is made however, these questions need to be asked. They could easily change the outcome.

Mephibosheth becomes the first winner; Ziba is the first loser. David gains appreciation and respect from Mephibosheth and contempt from the house of Ziba. This is the way life is. Your kindness to someone may be accepted by the recipient but rejected by a relative or some casual observer. The key to understanding someone's kindness is to understand what is in his or her heart. Jeremiah said, "The heart is deceitful above all things, and desperately wicked: who can know it?" (Jeremiah 17:9, nasb). Both the speaker and the listener must be receptive to the situation and the needs of the other. To be kind is not always an easy matter. To receive someone's kindness is not always easy to do. But it is a far better world when we give and receive kindness. "Is there anyone left from the house of Saul?" asked David. We must take the risk and ask the question. Is there someone you can be kind to today?

For Further Bible Study

1. How does Abraham's servant interpret kindness in this Genesis passage? (Genesis 24:1–14)

2. What does Rahab expect in the way of kindness from the spies Joshua sent to spy on her city? (Joshua 2:1–12)

3. Why did Saul repay kindness to the Kenites?

For Personal Growth

1. While kindness is not something everyone possesses, it is seen in everyday events. Look in your newspaper or in other media opportunities this week for acts of human kindness. Was this kind act an usual behavior or was this kindness the person's general way of behaving?

2. Who is a person you know that exhibits kindness in unique occasions and in special moments and situations? Write down a few of those times and then interview that person for a deeper look into their lifestyle for ways to improve your own.

3. Make a list of ways kindness can be expressed without using the word. Example: Sending a card to a person in the hospital, provide materials for a needy child in school, read to an elderly person.

THE QUEEN OF SHEBA SAID TO SOLOMON...

"YOU EXCEL IN WISDOM."

1 KINGS 10:7

SOMETIMES IT IS HUMBLING TO ADMIT YOUR FRIEND'S GREATNESS.

In Solomon's day it was tough to be a queen in a world where male leadership dominated. When a woman did arrive at greatness the last thing she wanted to do was admit some man was greater than she was. History tells us the queen of Sheba's domain was in Southern Arabia on the major land trade route from the Orient and the old Babylonian empire to Egypt and Africa. There is nothing known about this area to say with confidence that the culture favored a woman's leadership. As sure as you know anything about history, you know there were bound to have been conflicts with men over the question of her role as queen. Women must fight the battle for leadership and recognition in every generation. It is even more amazing how, when the word *woman* is mentioned, the subject spins off into all kinds of side issues. Two men were leaving a pub and one said, "You can't live with them and you can't live without them." "That's the way women are, pal," said the other. "Who is talking about women?" said the first. "I was talking about credit cards." We can be grateful that women in scripture held many leadership positions. It is also true that their leadership made the difference between success and failure in some situations.

Whether it was to impress Solomon with her greatness or to meet her own needs, scripture tells us the queen of Sheba, "…came to Jerusalem with a very large entourage, with camels carrying spices and very much gold and precious stones" (1 Kings 10:2, nasb). From the get-go she wanted Solomon to know that she was not some poor, unimportant leader of a small tribal clan somewhere down south. Her large travel band, many camels, and vast treasures spoke of her wealth and ability as a leader. She certainly wanted to make a good first impression. When she left, scripture says, "She gave the king a hundred and twenty talents of gold and a very great amount of spices and precious stones" (1 Kings 10:10, nasb). If Old Testament numbers can be believed, each gold talent weighed about seventy-five pounds. This meant she gave Solomon a total of 9,000 pounds of gold plus more spices than Solomon's court had ever seen. Having heard about Solomon's greatness

I WISH I'D SAID THAT

and wealth, she may have felt she needed to start out on equal footing. Such an attitude or belief could have turned out to be a mistake. But her wealth and splendor certainly gave her a grand entrance to Israel's king. There is so much information here that it boggles the mind to remember and consider all of it.

The human mind stores values in the frontal lobes. From them we gain our perceptions and attitudes about whom we select and choose as our friends. We may choose our friends for some personal skill or ability such as music, sports, or intelligence. Or our choice may be based on their personal appearance, language skills, or personal beauty. We may choose our friends for their discipline, free spirit, or whatever reason or circumstances the situation demands. However, my church friends may not be the same ones as my work or social friends even if we do share some common values together. Some people might think us odd or off base because we choose the friends we do, but no matter. They are friends and we intend to keep them as long as we hold some things in common. Friendships come when we bond our values with another's because we have some things in common. From the start of this relationship between Solomon and Sheba, wealth certainly was one factor they shared in common. Sheba came prepared to build on that identity.

The primary reason some people choose their friends is wealth. Wealth, whether it is authentic or not, has always symbolized achievement, stature, power, and influence. Someone may have all of these characteristics except wealth, and therefore are not considered on par with those who have it. The commonality of wealth allows us to choose other people, places for travel, and lifestyles that are not available without it. A newspaper article told about Hollywood moguls whose wealth led each to build larger more lavish homes than their neighbors. The article told about one mogul who reigned at the top by living in a 50,000 square foot home until the newest Hollywood mogul built his 56,000 square foot home. After all, what is wealth if you can't flaunt it before those who have less? Displaying wealth can be quite a game. And it usually puts you in a different circle of friends. Wealth determines where you live, how you live, and who your friends are. Which public or private schools your children attend is often determined by your wealth. It has long been reality that the clothing apparel, shoes, backpacks, or other personal items such as cell phones often are used to classify school children. For some, it is where their parents take them on vacation or how they are transported to and from school. My high school friends drove newer and better automobiles to school than their teachers. Teenagers still look down on the poor because of the "rags" they wear. The poor student seldom hangs out at the mall, goes on dates to fancy restaurants, or drives to out-of-town movies with the wealthy. One high school in Tennessee recently ended senior proms because the cost for luxury limos, fancy dinners, and after prom events became too expensive for the average family. Of course the opposite is true too. The poor are also attracted to wealth. Choosing wealthy friends presents difficulties for the poor. What to wear, where to go, and how to get there are difficult choices the wealthy do not have to worry about. Occasionally friendship between rich and poor happens even when parents seek the validity for such relationships. The contrast between the two is often easier to accept than explain.

Jesus had much to say about wealth and poverty and the great separation there is between the two. The widow with the two mites and the rich man and Lazarus are a couple of good examples where riches were a problem. So we may choose our friends for a variety of reasons. Most of us have few friends from high school or college days who have achieved star status. And of course those who did become stars are our friends now even if they were not then. Claiming them as old friends gives us reason to brag or tell stories that include us with the hope that our new friends will think us important. We may not have the old friend's singing voice or athletic ability, but to be associated with them somehow associates us with greatness.

I love to sing, but do not have a solo voice. I attended high school with Noel Paul Stookey of Peter, Paul, and Mary fame. We were in the same high school fraternity together. Our fraternity shared a joint meeting with a girls' fraternity, and Paul organized a singing group to help with the entertainment for the girls. He introduced each singer and told what part each sang. I was introduced as "singing background." It was an apt description because if I sang low enough in the background I might add "mass" to the other singers but not much quality. However, my lack of musical talent has never stopped me from claiming Noel's friendship. So it was with the queen of Sheba who came to test Solomon's wisdom and greatness with the hopes that they could become friends. Scripture says she couldn't believe what she had been told about his greatness. Sheba may have reasoned in her mind, *He just couldn't be that great, so I will go and see this guy.* Is there any doubt in your mind that when she returned to South Arabia she talked about her "rich new friend" in Israel? You know what you would have said; would she be any different? Not likely. If we are not stars, being associated with them in some way is good enough.

Friendships may start out on a negative note. Having a friend or being a friend doesn't mean it was or is a perfect relationship. We would like to think and believe that our own positive attributes far exceed our negative characteristics, but it may not be so. Sometimes there are negatives that must be accepted or even tolerated if the friendship is to last. One such negative is the way we use or abuse language. Wisdom often is tied to language skills. The queen of Sheba came with difficult questions to test Solomon's wisdom. While we might believe that testing another person's language and mind skill is a pretty negative way to build a friendship, I suggest to you it is often our first choice for a way to begin conversations that start a relationship. In Western culture it is standard practice to ask questions about what you do, where you live, or what position you hold in an organization. We generally share such information because it is the cultural norm to do so unless we are embarrassed or ashamed our answers will tell more about ourselves than we want known. For example, when new ministers meet, the usual conversation starts with "Where did you go to seminary?" This question is designed to answer several unasked questions. Is this person a seminary graduate or not? The answer tells you something about his or her education and training. Secondly, it may tell something about the person's theological point of view. Was the theological foundation at their seminary identified as a conservative, moderate, or liberal? If they tell you when and where they attended seminary you may discover you have a mutual friend or favorite professor in common. If however, they have not attended an accredited seminary, you may be tempted to form a negative opinion in your mind about their educational qualification for ministry. After introductions were made, Sheba may have said, "I have heard many things about your greatness. Who was your teacher?" She may have been looking for reasons for his greatness outside his personal skills and attributes. While education can be a bridge to friendship, it can also initiate icy words that separate people into the haves and have-nots. The same may be true with questions or statements about world travels or important meetings and events someone has attended. We throw these words out to see if people will be impressed. The queen of Sheba and Solomon both had things to be proud about. You can be sure that with gifts like they exchanged they knew a lot about the other before they ever laid eyes on one another.

Scripture tells us that Solomon "answered all her questions; nothing was hidden from the king which he did not explain to her" (1 Kings 10:3, nasb). Who among us would not enjoy such an opportunity to share such wisdom and testing? Most of us would relish the chance to share our knowledge with someone who really, really wants to know. These moments may have brought them together by the use of friendly banter and raillery. She asked, and he answered, and so it went with each question until she was satisfied that his reputation was not exaggerated. What may be perceived as a stressful and unwanted investigation by some may be seen as playful conversation rather than an intentional attack on one's credibility. It may be interesting to note that I have heard this passage preached both ways.

We know a lot more today about personality theory and interpersonal relations that help us make friendships. Extraverted people talk to think. Introverted people think to talk. Solomon is known for his many words. We know little about the queen other than what we have here in scripture. While Hollywood may have presented her as a beautiful coy woman, asking her questions while flashing her baby blue eyes or shaking her blond hair, in reality she may have had none of these characteristics and spoken with an interpreter. In such a situation the possibility for developing a quick friendship becomes more difficult because of the language barrier. Voice tones, smiles, body language, and eye contact can quickly conquer many language barriers to build a lasting friendship.

One's spirituality and relationship to God can help make a difficult situation pleasant. In this passage the historian chooses to say, "Nothing was hidden from the king," meaning that God fulfilled His promise to give Solomon wisdom as well as wealth. Wisdom can certainly be an asset when our conversation is tested. Could it be that Solomon sought the Lord's help before his conversation with Sheba? Certainly scripture tells us that beginning with his selection as Israel's new king he sought wisdom from God. Solomon's wisdom in Proverbs teaches us that the "fear of the Lord is the beginning of wisdom" (Proverbs 1:7, nasb). But there must be more here than wisdom, for we know at least one or more people who are wise but with whom we would never be counted as their friend. I like to think that Solomon's wisdom here was an asset rather than a hindrance. Gary Harbaugh writes in *God's Gifted People*, "In Psalm 139 we are given a powerful image of a God who knows us better than we know ourselves, a God who personally shapes us as individuals according to the Lord's own designs" (1990). To have wisdom and use it wisely is a problem for some people. Einstein was considered slow in school when in reality he was just bored.

This scripture passage closes with a declaration by the queen of Sheba about Solomon's greatness and the Lord's blessing upon his kingdom. She came to test him but discovered that his God was his teacher. She closes her praise saying, "Blessed be the Lord your God who delighted in you to set you on the throne of Israel; because the lord loved Israel forever, therefore, He made you king, to do justice and righteousness" (1 Kings 10:9, nasb).

When the queen of Sheba left Israel for home, she was humbled by her experience. Back home her power and wealth were unequaled. She was queen of her kingdom and none was greater. Now her journey brought a new experience about one who was greater than herself. This is not the same kind of experience you and I might have as we stand on the sidewalk and watch a presidential parade pass. Even though it may be the president of the United States and we respect him and the office he holds, it isn't the same as when we are invited to the Oval Office and spend enough time with him to ask our questions and get them answered.

Humility is a characteristic not found in many world leaders. Recently I watched a videotape of former President Jimmy Carter teaching his Sunday school class in Plains, Georgia. His presentation, demeanor, and concern for both his lesson material and his congregation spoke to me of his humility. He asked questions to involve his class. When he expressed his opinion as a world leader, he indicated his thoughts by saying, "I believe" and "this is what I think." There are characteristics that world leaders must have to achieve greatness, and some of these same characteristics are used to identify them as tyrants and dictators. Wisdom and humility are a sweet combination. Wealth and power can influence great leaders to make foolish decisions. The quality of a person's leadership cannot be separated from the depth of his or her character.

Whether history has correctly identified the queen of Sheba as a great leader we may never know more than what has already been written in scripture. She came to see Solomon as an equal. She was proud, prepared, and ready for a grand encounter. She achieved her stated goal to find out for sure if what was told her was reality. Solomon's presence, opulence, and grandeur exceeded anything she had ever known. In addition she left with a different point of view—his wisdom was a gift from his God. She recognized the spiritual value of God and acknowledged God's blessing upon Solomon.

Many of us wish for such an experience. But to whom would we go? Where can we find such wealth and wisdom? Could some Middle Eastern oil mogul equal Solomon's wealth? Maybe, but possibly not when compared to the times in which he lived. Could we find a man wiser than Solomon today? Yes, we probably could because there are more things to be wise about today than in Solomon's time. Sheba returned home wiser than when she left. Solomon's wealth and wisdom exceeded her expectation. In her response to Solomon, her declaration that God was behind it all may be just what we are searching for also. It is a humbling experience to realize that wisdom and wealth come from God who owns it all. The splendors of heaven will far exceed our understanding of what is wealth in this domain. And the words of our Lord are more than enough to keep us humble as we meditate on what are the important things that need considering when making friends. "Blessed be the Lord your God" (1 Kings 10:9, nasb). I wish I'd said that, don't you?

For Further Bible Study

1. In the book of Acts, who was a wealthy disciple, a missionary, and a friend all at the same time?

2. What differences stand out when you compare the lives of Samson and Delilah and King Solomon and the queen of Sheba?

3. What did Job's friends decide was cause for all of Job's troubles?

For Personal Growth

1. Name the characteristics you like about your best

friend. Do those same characteristics make you their best friend? Why or why not?

2. Have you ever examined or thought about the agenda behind questions you ask of people you talk to and know little about? Pay more attention next time and try to determine if your questions are searching for weakness in their character to extend your own or if you genuinely want to find things you have in common to deepen the conversation or relationship.

3. How much do you believe your life experiences, background, and social standing have to do with the number of friends you have? Why have you chosen them or why did they choose you?

EPILOGUE

Words! You have just read about 50,000 words in fifteen chapters from stories taken from the Old Testament about important and everyday people who said something that made a difference. May I suggest to you that they are not more gifted, talented, or braver than you or me? They were simply people who chose to be used for God at a particular moment in their lives to bring opportunity and blessings to someone else. It is not as if in life it has to be some unusual coincidence that allows God to use us. Rather it is a willingness on our part to be used, to be a blessing to someone else, to care enough to become involved. Did you get these ideas from each chapter? Dr. Cupp and I hope so.

First, using words that make a difference does require some understanding about how people think, live, and relate to one another. The good news is that most people are willing to let us build a relationship with them if we are willing to take the time and effort to make the relationship meaningful and positive. Second, no matter how much we try to conceal our emotions and feelings, how we express our words in tone and body language tell the listener more about our real intentions to build solid, loving, and lasting relationships. Third, behind every conversation is the storehouse of experiences in the human mind. From that storehouse of experience we give meaning, purpose, and intention to the words we use. We must never forget that the person who listens to our words must find some common meaning and agreement in the way we use our words for us to carry on a conversation. Finally, Christians can have what Paul writes about to the Church at Corinth and refers to as the spiritual man rather than the carnal man. Dying to Christ and discovering God's will for your life puts you as the speaker and the listener in a totally different situation. We who are in Christ know how to die to self, forgive, and give compassionately to meet the needs of another person whether that person is a part of the Kingdom of God or not. Therefore, it is not as much that we know all the rules of grammar and syntax in order to use words to build solid lasting relationships. The real rules come from the heart of the believer, and the syntax comes from a mind filled with the spirit and not the world. Education of course can help you use the right words, but right actions start with what you put into your mind and heart.

Dr. Cupp and I hope you have found your journey with us informative as we explored Old Testament characters that made a difference by what they said. If you found this book refreshingly challenging, it is our hope that it will help you get on that path that leads to building better relationships. And if so, maybe someday someone will write a book about people like you who have used words to change situations, improve relationships, and build paths that bring people into fellowship with the Master.

Jim Rennell, DMin
Jann Cupp, PhD

REFERENCES

INTRODUCTION

Deutscher, G. (2005). The Unfolding of Language. Henry Holt & Co., 21.

Glasser, W. (1974). Reality Therapy. A Seminar for counselors, clergy and mental health workers. Lexington, KY: Harper Collins, New York.

Hallock, D. (2007). The Week. 03/30/07. 23.

Huxley, A. (2007). Public Radio. "Word for the Wise Quote." 10/26/07

CHAPTER 1 - ELI SAID TO SAMUEL

Arendt, H. (2006). The Week. "Wit and Wisdom." 09/08/06. 19.

Carpenter, S. (2001). Monitor on Psychology, "Research confirms the virtue of 'sleeping on it.'" 32, 49–51.

Funk, R. W. & Ben-Dor I., (1962). The Interpreter's Dictionary of the Bible. "Lamps." 63–64.

Foulkes, D. (1996). Sleep, Dream research. 19(8), 609–624.

Gais, S. & Born, J. (2004). Declarative memory consolidation: Mechanisms acting during human sleep. Learning and Memory, 11, 679–685.

Horne, J. (1988). Why We Sleep. New York: Oxford University Press.

Huber, R., Ghilardi, M.F., Massimini, M., & Tononi, G. (2004). Local sleep and learning. Nature, 430, 78–81.

Kecklund, G., Akerstedt, T., & Lowden, A. (1997). Morning work: Effects of early rising on sleep and alertness. Sleep, 20(3), 215–223.

Lefton, L. A. (2000). Psychology: Seventh Edition. Boston, Mass.: Allyn and Bacon.

CHAPTER 2 - DAVID SAID TO SAUL

Bandura, A. (1978). The self-system in reciprocal determinism. American Psychologist. April. 344–357.

Bandura, A. (1997). Self-efficacy: The exercise of self-control. New York: Freeman.

Harris, S.M., & Halpin, G. (2002). Development and validation of the factors influencing pursuit of higher education questionnaire. Educational and Psychological Measurement, 62, 79–96.

Jaffe, E. (2004). At the height of its game. APS Observer, 17, 25–27.

Jung, C. (2006) "Everything that irritates us about others can lead us to an understanding of ourselves." The Week Magazine 08/25/06, 19.

Murphy, S.M. (1990). "Models of imagery in sport psychology: a review." Journal of Mental Imagery, 14, 153–172.

Reicher, S., Haslam, A. & Platow, M. Scientific American Mind. "The New Psychology of Leadership." August/September 2007. p. 26.

Smith, D. & Chapin, T. (2000). Spiritual Healing, 73–114. Psycho-Spiritual Publications, Madison, WI.

CHAPTER 3 - ELDERS SAID TO REHOBOAM

Action, L., (2004). Oxford Dictionary of Quotations. P. 1.

Author Unknown (1990). Reader's Digest. May. 9.

Butterfield, E.C., Nelson, T.O., & Peck, V. (1988). Developmental aspects of the feeling-of-knowing. Developmental Psychology, 24, 654–663.

Diamond, J. (2005). Collapse. How societies choose to fail or succeed. Viking Press.

Glasser, W. (1965). Reality Therapy. Harper Collins, New York.

Hart, J.T. (1965). Memory and the feeling-of-knowing experience. Journal of Educational Psychology, 56, 208–216.

Matlin, M.W. (1989). Cognition. Fort Worth: Harcourt Brace Jovanovich College Publishers.

Metcalf, J. (1986). "Feeling of knowing in memory and problem solving." Journal of Experimental Psychology: Learning, Memory, and Cognition, 12, 288–294.

Stanford D. (1990) Reader's Digest, April.

Sperling, G. (1960). "The information available in brief visual presentations." Psychological Monographs, 74, 1–29.

CHAPTER 4 - SERVANTS SAID TO NAAMAN

Author Unknown (1992). Our Daily Bread. A daily devotional guide for Aug. 24, 1992. Published by Radio Bible Class Ministries, Grand Rapids, MI.

Binns, C. (2007). Mind. The Hidden Power of Culture. August/September 2007, 9.

Bower, G.H. (1992). "How might emotions affect learning?" In S.A. Christianson (Ed.), Handbook of Emotion and Memory (pp. 3–31). Hillsdale, NJ: Erlbaum

Darke, S. (1988). "Anxiety and working memory capacity." Cognition and Emotion, 2, 145–154.

Ellis, H.C., & Ashbrook, P.W. (1988). Resource allocation model of the effects of depressed mood states on memory. In K. Fiedler & J. Forgas (Eds.), Affect, cognition, and social behavior. Toronto: Hogrefe.

Schacter, D.L., (1999). "The seven sins of memory: Insights from psychology and cognitive neuroscience." American Psychologist, 54, 182–203.

CHAPTER 5 - LEPERS SAID TO THE GATEKEEPERS

Brin, D. (2007). The Week. 12/07/07, 21.

Chaplin, J.P. (1985). Dictionary of psychology. NY: Laurel, 21.

Clarkson, P. (1996). To act or not to act: That is the question. London: Whurr.

Festinger, L. (1957). A theory of cognitive dissonance. Evanston, IL: Row, Peterson.

Fitts, P.M., & Posner, M.I. (1967). Human performance. Belmont, CA: Brooks Cole.

Henry, W. Chicago Tribune. (No date given.)

Hull, C. (1943). Principles of behavior. NY: Appleton-Century-Crofts.

Jenkins, I.H., Brooks, D.J., Nixon, P.D., Frackowiak, R.S.J., & Passingham, R.E. (1994). "Motor sequence learning: A study with positron emission tomography." Journal of Neuroscience, 14, 3775–3790.

Krebs, D. (1975). Empathy and altruism. Journal of Personality and Social Psychology, 32, 1134–1140.

Latane, B., & Rodin, J. (1969). "A lady in distress: Inhibiting effects of friends and strangers on bystander intervention." Journal of Experimental and Social Psychology, 5, 189–202.

Pastor's Conference, Moody Founder's Week Moody Bible Institute, Chicago, IL. February 1975.

Prairie Overcomer Magazine.

Warren, R. (2002). Purpose Driven Life. Grand Rapids, MI. Zondervan.

CHAPTER 6 - ELIJAH SAID TO ELISHA

McCarty, H. "Oh, How I Loved Her." The Columbia, South Carolina State Newspaper,

Columbia, SC June 15, 1999

McGraw, P. (1999). Life Strategies. Doing What Works, Doing What Matters. Hyperion Press. 211–226

Toinspire Inc. To Inspire Newsletter. quotes@toinspire. com.

CHAPTER 7 - ESTHER SAID TO MORDECAI

Bullard, G. (1996). Strategic Planning Seminar South Carolina Baptist Convention, Columbia, SC.

Disraeli, B (2008). The Week 01/18/08. 21.

Luce, C. B. (Unknown) Reader's Digest Magazine. Rochester, NY.

Sternberg, Robert J. (1996). Cognitive Psychology, NY: Harcourt Brace.

Tversky, Amos (1972). Elimination by Aspects: A Theory of Choice. Psychological Review, 79, 281–299.

Toinspire Inc. (2004). To Inspire Newsletter. quotes@ toinspire.com. 05/13/04.

Wadsworth, B.J. (1996). Piaget's Theory of Cognitive and Affective Development (5th ed.). White Plains, NY: Longman.

Encyclopedia Wikipedia. The free encyclopedia. (9 December 2007) http://en.wikipedia.org/wikiClare_ Boothe_Luce

www.thisdaysa.co.za

CHAPTER 8 - SOLOMON SAID TO HIS SERVANT

Associated Press. (2004). "Mother Used Lock of Hair to Prove Girl's Identity." Fox News. (March 03, 2004) http://www.foxnews.com

Author Unknown (1993). Proclaim Magazine.

Author Unknown (1981) Reader's Digest Magazine. "Laughter, The Best Medicine." June 1981

Johnson, D. (2004). "Policing a Rural Plague." Newsweek 8 March 2004. 4.

Kennedy, John F. Profiles of Courage. Harper & Row Publishers, 1956. 136–156.

Snyder, C. (1990). Proclaim Magazine. Sunday School Board of the Southern Baptist Convention. Nashville, Tennessee. January 1990.

Warden, R. "Double-talk Fools Experts," of CBN "Mathematical Game Theory as Applied to Physical Education." CBN. March 5, 2004.

CHAPTER 9 - NEHEMIAH SAID TO THE WORKERS

Author Unknown (2001). Time Magazine. June 18, 2001. 45.

Bullard, G. (March 12, 1996) Strategic Planning Seminar South Carolina Baptist Convention, Columbia, SC.

Broadman Commentary, Vol. 3, "Ezra-Nehemiah." Emmett W. Hamrick. Broadman Press 1970. 424.

Folkman, S. & Lazarus, R.S. (1980). An analysis of coping in a middle-aged community. Sample. Journal of Health and Social Behavior, 21, 219–239.

Gladwell, M. (2005). Blink, The Power of Thinking Without Thinking. Little Brown and Company. New York.

Mufson, M. (2006), A Special Health Report from Harvard Medical School. "Coping with Anxiety and Phobias," Harvard Health Publications. 16.

Piper, D. (2004). 90 minutes in Heaven. Grand Rapids: Revell. 137.

Roosevelt, F. (1933). The Public Papers of Franklin D. Roosevelt. Volume Two: The Year of Crisis, 1933 New York: Random He, 1938. 11–16.

Zeitlin, S. (1980). Assessing coping behavior. American Journal of Orthopsychiatry, 50, 139–144.

CHAPTER 10 - ELISHA SAID TO THE PROPHET'S WIFE

Our Daily Bread, December 15, 1991. This illustration is from my card file. The date is unknown.

Quotation #1688. Laura Moncur's Motivational Quotations. http://www.quotationspage.com/quote/1688.html

CHAPTER 11 - RUTH SAID TO NAOMI

Author Unknown. (Our Daily Bread, July 14, 1986).

Author Unknown. Proclaim Magazine. April 1991

Bennett, H. "What Is Needed to Inspire Others?" Outreach Magazine. 04/1989. 39.

Carnegie, D. The Week 12/28/07. 21.

Chesborough, A. E-mail. Buy Her What She Wants! 08/20/05.

Hart, J. The Nashville Tennessean.

Henry, W. Chicago Tribune.

Schlessinger, L. How Could You Do That? Quoted in Peachtree Presbyterian Pulpit 05/03/98

Schwarzkopf, N. To Inspire Newsletter. April 24, 2002.

Truman, H. Brainy Quotes. http://www.brainyquote.com/quotes/quotes/h/harrystru109615.html

January 17, 2008.

CHAPTER 12 - JONATHAN SAID TO DAVID

Dye, P. Farmer's Almanac.

Emerson, R. (2008) quotes@toinspire.com.

Franklin, C. (2001) A quote received by e-mail on 05/17/01 from a friend.

Tilley, W. (1992). The Surpassing of Righteousness. Chapter 9, "Surpassing Law: Adultery and Swearing" Smyth and Helwys Press. 96.

CHAPTER 13 - ABIGAIL SAID TO DAVID

Broughton, L.

Oates, W. Proclaim Magazine

CHAPTER 14 - DAVID SAID TO MEPHIBOSHETH

Author unknown. Proclaim Magazine. Jan. 1985. 40.

Fields, W. (1968) The Baptist Program. Published by Exec Committee, SBC Convention, Nashville, TN August 1968. 30.

Good Stuff Magazine Progressive Business Publications Malvern, PA. 02/2005.

Pinker, S. (1997) How the Mind Works. Scientific American, W.W. Norton & Company, Inc., New York. 398.

Fields, W. The Baptist Program, Aug. 1968. Perspective by W.C. Fields, 30.

Tober, B. (2007) The Week. 11/09/07. 21.

CHAPTER 15 - QUEEN OF SHEBA SAID TO SOLOMON

Harbaugh, G.L. (1990). God's Gifted People. Augsburg Press, Minneapolis, MN. 21

FOR FURTHER BIBLE STUDY AND FOR PERSONAL GROWTH ANSWERS

CHAPTER 1: ELI SAID TO SAMUEL

For Further Bible Study

1. Answers: The baker and cupbearer—Genesis 40:8ff; Pharaoh—Genesis 41:15; King Nebuchadnezzar—Daniel 2:1

2. Answers: Abimelech—Genesis 20:3; Laban—Genesis 31:24; and Joseph's brothers—Genesis 37:5

3. Answers: Joseph—Genesis 41:15; Priscilla and Aquila—Acts 18:26

For Personal Growth

1. Answer: Did you change the words using terms familiar to a child? Did you demonstrate, draw a picture, or use a visual to guide the child's thinking? Remember some people need just a different word or picture to get them started in the right direction.

2. Answer: Your response.

3. Answer: Your response.

CHAPTER 2: DAVID SAID TO SAUL

For Further Bible Study

1. Answer: Abishai, Sebbecai, Elhanan, and Jonathan—2 Samuel 21:15–22
2. Answer: trumpets, pitchers, torches, and shouting.—Judges 7:20
3. Answer: a dog—1 Samuel 17:43

For Personal Growth

1. 1. Answer: Your response.
2. 2. Answer: Your response.
3. 3. Answer: Your search.

CHAPTER 3: ELDERS SAID TO REHOBOAM

For Further Bible Study

1. Answer: Joab, Barzillai, and Shimei—1 Kings 2:5–9
2. Answer: Your comparison
3. Answer: No! Read 1 Kings 12–14 for a record of his other failures.

For Personal Growth

1. Answer: Your story.
2. Answer: Your written record.
3. Answer: Your research.

CHAPTER 4: SERVANTS SAID TO NAAMAN

For Further Bible Study

1. Answer: Your response.
2. Answer: Your comparison.
3. Answer: He pointed out that the judgment he had pronounced on the guilty person was really a judgment upon himself.

For Personal Growth

1. Answer: Your research.
2. Answer: Your research and response.
3. Answer: Your response.

CHAPTER 5: LEPERS SAID TO GATEKEEPERS

For Further Bible Study

1. Answer: Yes! Pharaoh's daughter had access to power to make it happen.—Exodus 2:6.
2. Answers: Joseph, No—Genesis 21:45

3. Answer: Gideon's army used trumpets, torches, and pictures—Judges 7:1ff.

For Personal Growth

1. Answer: Your own story.
2. Answer: Don't give money, take them to a restaurant and buy them a meal and watch them eat it.
3. Answer: Your research.

CHAPTER 6: ELIJAH SAID TO ELISHA

For Further Bible Study

1. Answer: Your research and words.
2. Answer: Your response.
3. Answer: Your response.

For Personal Growth

1. Answer: Your decision.
2. Answer: Your response.
3. Answer: Your research.

CHAPTER 7: ESTHER SAID TO MORDECAI

For Further Bible Study

1. Answer: No, even pagans and unbelievers fast in the hope of getting what they want.

2. Answer: Yes. Both were angry and wanted to eliminate those who disagreed with them because they didn't get what they wanted for themselves.

3. Answer: The three commissioners and 120 satraps in Daniel 6.

For Personal Growth

1. Answer: Your response.
2. Answer: Your response.
3. Answer: Your response.

CHAPTER 8: SOLOMON SAID TO HIS SERVANT

For Further Bible Study

1. Answer: Eight, nine, and ten—Exodus 20:15–17
2. Answer: Elisha—2 Kings 4:18
3. Answer: It could be the idolatry he allowed to go on under his reign. God hates idolatry—1 Kings 11:1

For Personal Growth

1. Answer: Your response.
2. Answer: Martin Luther and Roger Williams
3. Answer: Your research and response.

CHAPTER 9: NEHEMIAH SAID TO THE WORKERS

For Further Bible Study

1. Answer: Matthew 6:25–34
2. Answer: Your response.
3. Answer: Be strong and of good courage.

For Personal Growth

1. Answer: Your response.
2. Answer: Allergies, anxiety, depression, diabetes, heartburn, hypertension, colds, irritable bowel syndrome, ulcers, etc.
3. Answer: A prayer, retreat away from the crowds for a while to refocus on your mission.

CHAPTER 10: ELISHA SAID TO THE PROPHET'S WIFE

For Further Bible Study

1. 1. Answer: Your response.
2. 2. Answer: Eutychus—Acts 20:9
3. 3. Answer: Your response.

For Personal Growth

1. Answer: Your response
2. Answer: Your research and response.

3. Answer: Your response and action.

CHAPTER 11: RUTH SAID TO NAOMI

For Further Bible Study

1. Answer: Your choice.
2. Answer: Your thoughts.
3. Answer: Not willing at first, but did as the Lord requested and brought him to Damascus.—Acts 9:10–22

For Personal Growth

1. Answer: Your thoughts. Is there an illustration here worth sharing with others when the right moment comes?
2. Answer: Your response.
3. Answer: Your research.

CHAPTER 12: JONATHAN SAID TO DAVID

For Further Bible Study

1. Answer: John, Mark, 2 Timothy 4:11, and Colossians 4:10
2. Answer: Your response.
3. Answer: Your study notes.

For Personal Growth

1.   Answer: Your response.
2.   Answer: Your response.
3.   Answer: Your research.

CHAPTER 13: ABIGAIL SAID TO DAVID

For Further Bible Study

1.   Answer: Your response.
2.   Answer: Jezebel
3.   Answer: Jacob's advice to his sons for restoring a relationship with their brother Joseph.

For Personal Growth

1.   Answer: Your response.
2.   Answer: Your response.
3.   Answer: Your research.

CHAPTER 14: DAVID SAID TO MEPHIBOSHETH

For Further Bible Study

1.   Answer: The person who shows kindness to his master's animals and himself is the one whom God has chosen as Isaac's bride.
2.   Answer: Protection for herself and her household.

3. Answer: For their kindness to Israel during the Exodus.—1 Samuel 15:6

For Personal Growth

1. Answer: Your research.
2. Answer: Your investigation.
3. Answer: Your list.

CHAPTER 15: QUEEN OF SHEBA SAID TO SOLOMON

For Further Bible Study

1. Answer: Barnabas, Acts 4:36, 15:37.
2. Answer: Samson and Delilah's relationship was based on lust and worldly gain. Solomon and Sheba's friendship was based on mutual respect and admiration.
3. Answer: He was righteous in his own eyes. Job 32:1

For Personal Growth

1. Answer: Your response.
2. Answer: Your own study.
3. Answer: your response.

TEACHING PROCEDURES

FIVE THINGS TO REMEMBER BEFORE YOU BEGIN TO TEACH

1. Prepare yourself spiritually to teach. Teaching is not just an opportunity to say something. It is an investment of the resources and gifts God has entrusted you to strengthen those He sends to you for growth. (James 3:1–2)

2. There is no substitute for knowing the needs of your class members. Build a notebook on each person who attends. Beside names, addresses, and phone numbers, know their strengths and weaknesses. Can they pray? Do they know their Bible? Are there habits and attitudes they need to change? Pray for them and develop a lesson plan that meets their needs, not yours.

3. Don't wait until the night before or day of your class to begin your preparation. Begin as soon as

you finish each lesson by writing down what you remember about your last class and add notes to each member's history (#2 above). Turn the pages in your notebook and pray for each member. Collect and keep extra Bibles in your classroom for visitors to use.

4. Teach by a humble example of what it means to be forgiven, redeemed, and commissioned to serve our risen Lord. It is not your wisdom that changes another's point of view. You are only the vehicle God's spirit uses to get the job done. People model great teachers. Be the greatest teacher you can be without compromise or a false humility.

5. Ask often for your class to give a testimony when changes and opportunities have come to them and they have found victory. Create a fire that will lead others to want to catch the vision. People grow when their lifestyles change. Don't neglect your preparation. Know the answers to the questions at the end of the chapter so when students ask, you are prepared.

HOW TO USE THESE TEACHING PROCEDURES

1. You are not obligated to use part or all of the suggestions and are quite free to adapt the lesson procedures to fit the needs of your class. These proce-

dures are aimed at a forty-five minute to one hour teaching period.

2. The teaching outline is structured in the same way for every lesson to give continuity to the teaching process. It helps students to become comfortable and know what to expect and how to prepare for your leadership.

3. You may want to bring in a special guest from time to time and use a dialogue methodology between you and the guest expert. Pastors, deacons, other church or community leaders may have special gifts that can make your class exciting by providing experience with your topic.

4. It is okay to teach Bible history, but give the Holy Spirit a chance to work in the lives of your class members. Point out to students that they should seek an "aha" moment when the light comes on and they realize the Lord is giving them something to consider, think about, or change in their lifestyle.

5. Some students may want to make a journal and others may not. Make every effort to get students to answer the questions at the end of each chapter. The goal is to help them grow spiritually by providing them with evidence and a record of events and opportunities for service and ministry.

6. Look at the evaluation sheet before you prepare

your first lesson. Know what you want to accomplish before you start. Focus your teaching procedures on the goals you choose and then evaluate your success/failure so that next time you can improve your teaching. Revise the evaluation sheet if necessary to match your teaching goals and aims.

7.   May the joy of the Lord go with you and bless your ministry,

---

TEACHING PROCEDURES

CHAPTER 1: ELI SAID TO SAMUEL

Lesson aim: How to improve your rest. (Write aim on shelf/butcher paper or chalk board).

Text: 1 Samuel 3:9. Additional scripture resources to read in advance: Genesis 2:2, Joshua 1:13, Psalm 37:7, 116:7, Jeremiah 6:16, Matthew 11:29, 2 Corinthians 2:13 (*).

Preparation: Ask someone you know and trust to be prepared to give a (5–10) testimony on their meditation lifestyle and practices. Use them at (**) this point or one of your own choosing.

Preparation: Have magic markers, paper, and resources on meditation, spiritual rest, and private devotional times. Ask for recommendations from your pastor, church librarian, and local Christian bookstores. Prepare a handout if you have the resources or write names and telephone numbers on shelf-paper and tack it up where the class can refer to it if they are interested.

TEACHING OUTLINE:

Open with prayer and then quote lesson aim. Point out how important it is to know what scripture teaches us about any subject before we start talking about it.

I. What does the scripture say? (Lay down a biblical base for discussion and later decisions.)

*Lead a discussion: "Let's look at some Bible references that have something to say about rest." (Use those selected above or others you choose from a concordance. Write verses on shelf-paper, chalk board, or butcher paper so class members can easily find them with you.)

Ask: "How is the word rest used in the context of this passage?" (Go on to the next verse.)

Ask: "Did anyone find the answers to the Further Bible Study questions at the end of this chapter?" (Go over the three questions and/or find answers. The goal is to get students to read the text and do additional Bible study on their own to prepare for each class session.)

Summary: "It appears scriptures takes rest seriously and makes it more than sleep."

II. How can we apply this great Bible passage to our life today?

Ask: "What are some words we use to refer to rest?" (Crashed, died, couldn't wake up, etc.)

Ask: "What kind of sleep did the text writers talk about?" (Refer to passages you select.)

Ask: "In your opinion do you think most Christians know how to spiritually rest? Why?"

Ask: "Can anyone share with us a time when they had a spiritual rest/sleep and the Lord revealed something unique, special, or answers a question for you in your rest?" (Do several.)

**State: "I have asked (name) to share with us how they find spiritual rest and mediate."

Summary: "If scripture teaches it, do you think we should consider it?"

III. Where is my challenge to spend time with God in meditation and spiritual rest?

Share: "I have asked several people to recommend good books, articles, and reading on this subject and I would like to consider reading more about this important topic with this handout."

Remind your class of the lesson aim and close in prayer.

TEACHING PROCEDURES

CHAPTER 2: DAVID SAID TO SAMUEL

Lesson aim: The Lord has a place for you. (Write aim on shelf/ butcher paper or chalk board.)

Text: 1 Samuel 17:32. Additional scriptures to read: Saul—1 Samuel 16:14–23 David—1 Samuel 10–17

Preparation: Call one class member each week and ask him/her to pray for you and your class a couple of times during the week. Let them know you are depending on the Lord for this work.

TEACHING OUTLINE:

Review: Ask if anyone had a victory with spiritual rest and meditation this week. (2–3 minutes.)

Open with prayer and then quote lesson aim. Point out again how important it is to know what scripture teaches us about any subject before we start talking about it.

I. What does the scripture say? (Lay down a biblical base for discussion and later decisions.)

Ask: "What reasons do people give for not serving God?" (Handicaps, fear, education, etc.)

Ask: "What does Chapter 17 teach us about David?" (His brothers are in Saul's army (13). He is the youngest son of Jesse (14, 33). His mission is to take food and bring news (15–20). He lacked military experience (38–40). He is courageous (32, 45–47). Add other passages.)

Ask: "If you were a recruiter for Saul's army would this young man be a good candidate?"

Summarize: "What do you think could have happened if David had not answered God's call?"

II. How can we apply this great Bible passage to our life today?

Ask: "What kind of giants are we facing in our world today?" (List class members' responses on chalk board/butcher paper. Economic giants, lack of trust in CEO's, rising cost of an education, declining morals and values. See text for other examples.)

State: "What problems would an impulsive person have finding God's will for their life? What are some of the reasons listed in our text that show us David was not impulsive?" (List on paper.)

Ask: "How did David's self-confidence help him understand his call?"

1. David had God's anointing. (We are doomed to fail without making God's will ours.)

2. David had training and experience. (Trained servants have opportunity and priority.)

3. David had courage to stand up for his nation and against her enemies. (His lifestyle and values gave him the courage he needed and God's anointing provided the rest.)

Summarize: "God's people are fighting giants today that are just as big as Goliath!" Where does the Lord want you to serve? Maybe he is calling you right now? How would you know?

III. Where is my challenge to serve and how have I responded?

Ask: "Who could be a model or mentor for you if you wanted to grow spiritually and be used in the Lord's army?"

Remind your class of the lesson aim and close in prayer.

TEACHING PROCEDURES

CHAPTER 3: ELDERS SAID TO REHOBOAM

Lesson aim: How can I gain wisdom? (Write aim on shelf/ butcher paper or chalk board.)

Text: 1 Kings 12:1–17. Additional scripture to read: 2 Chronicles 1:10, Psalm 51:6, Proverbs 1:7

Preparation: Ask someone you know who usually makes wise decisions to join your class. (*)

TEACHING OUTLINE:

Review: Ask if anyone had a victory understanding God's call on his/her life this past week.

Open with prayer and then quote lesson aim. Point out again how important it is to know what scripture teaches us about any subject before we start talking about it.

I. What does the scripture say? (Lay down a biblical base for discussion and later decisions.)

State: "Plato said what most of us have experienced...'Wise folks speak when they have something to say, and fools talk when they have to say something.' Is this your habit?"

Ask: "Name a Bible character who was wise or foolish and tell us why you think so."

Ask: "Who were the wise and who were the fools in our Bible text for today? Why?"

*Ask: "Call on your guest or ask someone for their usual method for making wise decisions?"

Summary: "Scripture then has much to say about the wise and foolish. We all have and known people who had to say something instead of having something to say. How do you learn to be a better listener, say and do wiser things?"

II. How can we apply this great Bible passage to our life today?

State: "Find the William Glasser quote on page (14)? Now, how can we develop habits and attitudes that will not lead us just to believe we are right, but to do and say the right things?"

List: Students responses: (Develop good listening skills. Think and pray by asking the Lord for help before you speak. Learn to use silence or a pause as a response. Learn to say no or I am not sure and I need to think about that before I can give you a good answer. Use good logic.)

Ask: "What mistakes did Rehoboam make in his thinking process?" (List them on board/paper.)

Ask: "What role does perception play in decision making?" See Cupp text page (54)

Ask: "What author's suggestions about building better relationships do you like on page (57)?"

Ask: "In your opinion is Jung's statement on that same page at the bottom true?"

Ask: "In the Personal Growth section question #2 and explain what you think Dr. Cupp means?"

Ask: "Is it fair then to say that wise people then have

taken the effort and made the sacrifice to store and remember experiences that are going to be beneficial for them in their daily lifestyle?"

Summary: How does Bible study help us do that? (We learn the right morals and values.)

III. Where is my challenge to find Godly wisdom and use it for spiritual growth?

Ask: "Where can you go to find more help additional wisdom resources. (Make suggestions.)

Remind your class of the lesson aim and close in prayer.

TEACHING PROCEDURES

CHAPTER 4: SERVANTS SAID TO NAAMAN

Lesson aim: Can anger be controlled? (Write aim on shelf/ butcher paper or chalk board.)

Text: 2 Kings 5:10–14 Additional scripture: God—Exodus 4:14, Man—Genesis 4:5, Luke 4:28.

Preparation: Look in newspapers for stories about anger to use if you want others. (*)

Teaching Outline:

Review: Can anyone share with us a time in the past week when you prayed for wisdom?

Open with prayer and then quote lesson aim. Point out

again how important it is to know what the scripture teaches us about any subject before we start talking about it.

I. What does the scripture say? (Lay down a biblical base for discussion and later decisions.)

Ask: "How dangerous was it in Bible days to speak out as a slave? (Slaves had little value.)

Ask: "What mistakes were made in this story that lead up to the disaster of Naaman's anger?" (List: He made false assumptions. He tried to bribe Elisha. He used past experiences for a new situation. He forgot his common sense. Unaware he crossed cultural/theological boundaries.)

Ask: "Did anyone make a comparison of Naaman and Gehazi?" Further Bible Study #2 (Gehazi lied to Naaman to get what he shouldn't have. Naaman was obedient and was healed.)

Summary: "What we say and how we say it does make a difference. However, in the end we may find that what we wanted is not God's will and we suffer the consequences."

II. How can we apply this great Bible passage to our life today?

Ask: "How difficult is it today to talk logic or common sense to someone who is angry? Why?"

Ask: "What does it mean to "get your ego in the way of a decision?" (Selfish to get your way.)

*Ask: "Use an author's illustration on pages (67-71). Pick a partner to discuss one example. In five minutes I will ask for some to share their examples when someone used anger to get what they wanted."

Ask: "Is it wrong for a parent/supervisor to angrily discipline a child/adult for angry behavior?"

Ask: "If we know anger creates problems why do we use it so often to solve a problem?" (List: It worked once. We saw someone else use it. We learned it from our parents/boss. It's natural.)

Summary: "Anger is a solution, but usually not the best one. We learn to control our anger when we get our pride and ego out of the situation and look for facts and information that will make a problem a win/win situation for all. Scripture and our present world is filled with angry people all trying to get their own way. Saying and doing the right things rules out angry behavior."

III. Where is my challenge to serve and how have I answered?

Ask: "Where could you go to get help with your anger? If you know someone's temper keeps him/her from living the Christian life they desire, could you name someone who might help?"

Remind your class of the lesson aim and close in prayer.

TEACHING PROCEDURES

CHAPTER 5: LEPERS SAID TO THE GATEKEEPERS

Lesson aim: We can change our perceptions? (Write aim on shelf/ butcher paper or chalk board.)

Text: 2 Kings 7:10 Additional scripture: Leviticus 13. Matthew 6:22, 8:2, 18:9, Luke 17:12

Preparation: Research perception for examples so you clearly understand the differences. (*)

TEACHING OUTLINE:

Review: Can anyone share with us a time last week when someone controlled their anger?

Open with prayer and then quote lesson aim. Point out again how important it is to know what the scripture teaches about any subject before we start talking about it.

I. What does the scripture say? (Lay down a biblical base for discussion and later decisions.)

Ask: "Where in the Bible does the Lord give guidance about leprosy? (Leviticus 13.)

Ask: "What diseases today are comparable with leprosy?" (AIDS, Dengue Fever, Ebola)

*Ask: "What perceptions were going on that gave such different views on what to do?" (Syrians perceived they were in ultimate danger and fled. Lepers perceived they were being selfish. The king perceived the Syrians were hiding. The servants perceived someone should go see.)

Ask: "Were any of these perceptions wrong or just from a different point of view?" (Use this same idea to answer the following questions about who perceived what. Pick one or two.)

- David's idea on how to fight Goliath verses Saul's idea of how to fight him. I Samuel 17

- Jesus' idea about the tables of the money changers verses the Jewish leaders view. John 2:14

- Paul's idea verses Barnabas' idea of why John Mark should go or not go again. Acts 15:37

Summary: Your perceptions or point of view determines how you respond and what kind of decisions you make. Making the wrong perception is just as easy to do today as in Bible days.

II. How can we apply this great Bible passage to our life today?

Ask: "Look at Rick Warren's comment in our text on page (85). What does he mean by 'over-commitment to the wrong things'?" (Greed, lust, self-serving morals and values.) See I John 1:6–10 for the Bible's answer. (We need to be discerning about what the world offers us.)

Ask: "In your opinion what is the purpose of advertising?" (Change perceptions about a product.)

*Ask: "Advertising is aimed at getting people to believe something is true. Is this any different from the perceptions in our Bible passage?" (None, they all believed their own thinking.)

Ask: "Is there a methodology to use to change a point of view or perception?" (Yes, look at problems, situations, or issues from everyone point of view and determine which is best.)

III. Where is my challenge to serve and how have I answered?

Ask: Do you have a discerning spirit or are you easily persuaded? What can you do to change?

Remind your class of the lesson aim and close in prayer.

TEACHING PROCEDURES

CHAPTER 6: ELIJAH SAID TO ELISHA

Lesson aim: How to get what you ask for. (Write aim on shelf/butcher paper or chalk board.)

Text: 2 Kings 2:9 Additional scripture: Judges 7, 1 Samuel 1, 1 Kings 3

Preparation: Get a Bible dictionary and research Elijah and Elisha's lives (*).

TEACHING OUTLINE:

Review: Did anyone this week have any success trying to change your perceptions?

Open with prayer and then quote lesson aim. Point out again how important it is to know what the scripture teaches us about any subject before we start talking about it.

I. What does the scripture say? (Lay down a biblical base for discussion and later decisions.)

Ask: "Name someone who had a mentor/student relationship?" (Paul/Timothy.)

Ask: "One page (95) find a trait Elisha had that got him what he wanted?" (Perseverance.)

Ask: "How did Elisha know that he was chosen to be Elijah's replacement?" (2 Kings 2:15.)

Ask: "Can you recall where Jesus taught about a woman who had perseverance?" (Luke 18:1–8.)

*Ask: Call on someone who answered Further Bible Study question #1. (Add your research.)

Ask: "In your opinion was Elisha after greatness or service? Why?" (Service—work was hard.)

Ask: "Is the author's summary of Elisha's work correct? (105-106) What would you add?"

Summary: "We must continually ask ourselves about our motives for anything we do. Is our work to make money or provide a good product for the price? Do we seek our own fame for ourselves or do we share that success with others? We must measure success by biblical standards."

II. How can we apply this great Bible passage to our life today?

Ask: "How did the man outside the video store measure success?" (If he could save just one.)

Ask: "How did the man in the tollbooth measure success?" (It was a job he loved doing.)

Ask: "If you were to choose a mentor for your life who would it be and why?"

Ask: "What does our author quoting Dr. Phil say you must have to find success?" (A goal.)

State: "Is this true? If you do not have a goal you are helping someone else with theirs."

Ask: "How would you measure your life to determine if you are successful?"

Summary: "Elisha might not be our most favored Bible

person, but he certainly knew what he wanted in order to be Elijah's successor. You may not model your after someone else's but you must have a goal, a standard of measurement or else you will be pressured to go in every direction and help only help other accomplish their goals."

III. Where is my challenge to serve and how have I answered?

Ask: "Where might you find someone to talk to about your lifestyle, career, or future?"

Remind your class of the lesson aim and close in prayer.

TEACHING PROCEDURES

CHAPTER 7: ESTHER SAID TO MORDECAI

Lesson aim: Is self-sacrifice necessary? (Write aim on shelf/ butcher paper or chalk board.)

Text: Esther 4:16 Additional scripture: Ephesians 5:21ff, Hebrews 13:17, 1 Peter 5:5

Preparation: On the internet, find articles fasting and a self-sacrificing attitude (*).

TEACHING OUTLINE:

Review: Did anyone do some research on their career or their mentor from last week's lesson?

Open with prayer and then quote lesson aim. Point out again how important it is to know what the scripture teaches about the subject before we start talking about it.

I. What does the scripture say? (Lay down a biblical base for discussion and later decisions.)

Ask: "Who was Esther and how did she become queen?" (Esther 2.)

Ask: "What was the crisis that brought her to make plans for a banquet?" (Esther 3, 4, & 5.)

*Ask: "What does our text say about fasting. Have any of you ever had a spiritual fast?"

Ask: "List words that describe Haman's behavior and character." (List on board/newsprint.)

Do last week's words like career success, goals, and achievement fit Haman efforts this week?

Ask: "What differences are there between the perceptions of Haman, Mordecai, and Esther?"

Summary: "Situations such as this are often confusing, sometimes dangerous and seldom easy to solve. All of this could have been avoided if Haman had been a man who served others rather than himself.

When our goal is to take care of number one, we usually abuse people to succeed."

II. How can we apply this great Bible passage to our life today?

Ask: "List some major problems in our country as you understand them." (List on chalkboard.)

Ask: "Do you agree that behind each of us there is a person(s) who is selfish, greedy, and full of false pride, has a lust for power, or are angry and an unwillingness work out a better solution?"

Ask: "If you were in Esther's situation today would you consider fasting as a start? Why?"

*Ask: "How does fasting/prayers help anyone to find a solution or solve a difficult problem?"

Ask: "If you wanted God's help with a problem, where would you start?" (With yourself.)

Ask: "Is self-sacrifice necessary for success whether for you, your church, or your nation? (Yes.)

Summary: "For those who choose a spiritual life style, self-sacrifice is a part of the process and moves the believer toward accomplishing God's plan for your life. Jesus said we must first die to self and then we can come and follow him. But it is difficult many Christians to die to self in order to be used for God's work in these times."

III. Where is my challenge to serve and how have I answered?

Ask: "Consider fasting for six hours or half a day while meditating and/or praying as a trial."

Remind your class of the lesson aim and close in prayer.

TEACHING PROCEDURES

CHAPTER 8: SOLOMON SAID TO HIS SERVANT

Lesson aim: Where is wisdom found? (Write aim on shelf/butcher paper or chalk board.)

Text: 1 Kings 3:24 Additional scripture: Job 28:12–28, Ecclesiastes 1:13ff, Acts 6:10.

Preparation: Call a class member and ask them to think about someone whose lifestyle reflected a deep spiritual commitment to share with your class. Use with either question marked (*).

TEACHING OUTLINE:

Review: Did any of you last week have an opportunity to see self-sacrifice in someone?

Open with prayer and then quote lesson aim. Point out again how important it is to know what the scripture teaches us about any subject before we start talking about it.

I. What does the scripture say? (Lay down a biblical base for discussion and later decisions.)

Ask: "Why was the dead child's mother so deceitful?" (She stole a child from his real mother.)

Ask: "How easy was it for you to identify with the real mother? Why?" (Her actions are right.)

Ask: "Does the occupation of the women have any bearing on the story or its outcome?" (No.)

Ask: "What gift did Solomon have that brought him to the right conclusion?" (Discernment.)

Ask: "Compare Solomon's decision to cut the child in half with the mother's to steal the child."

Ask: "Was the real mother's decision to give the child up realistic, considering her occupation?"

Summary: "Life is filled with difficult choices. The wise will make them even if they are painful."

II. How can we apply this great Bible passage to our life today?

Ask: "How did you view the mother in the story of the child supposedly lost in the fire?"

Ask: "What role does courage play in these three mothers?" (One is selfish and two are not)

Ask: "How is the selfish mother's behavior similar to CEO's, stockbrokers, and ball players."

Ask: "What is the difference in a mistake in judgment and a premeditated plan to deceive?"

Ask: "What example does the author give as an example of how easy it is to deceive people?" (131)

Ask: "Why do you think most people are satisfied without searching for Godly wisdom."

*Ask: "Let's look at question #2 in For Personal Growth. How did you answer that?"

*Ask: "Who is someone you think has Godly wisdom in your lifetime?"

Summary: "We often associate wisdom with education, however all intelligent people are not wise in their actions or behavior. Scripture tells us wisdom comes from God."

III. Where is my challenge to serve and how have I answered?

State: "Solomon prayed for wisdom and God gave it to him. Is this a good place for us to begin as well? How can we use spiritual wisdom in our daily communication with others this week?"

Remind your class of the lesson aim and close in prayer.

TEACHING PROCEDURES

CHAPTER 9: NEHEMIAH SAID TO THE WORKERS

Lesson aim: How can we overcome fear? (Write aim on shelf/ butcher paper or chalk board.)

Text: Nehemiah 4:14 Additional scripture: Genesis 3:8, Daniel 5:6, Matthew 14:27ff.

Preparation: Use internet to discover one fear not listed in the text, write it paper keep it hidden and use it at (*). Prepare a list of fears you might have had if you were one of the exiles (**).

TEACHING OUTLINE:

Review: Did you do some observations and thinking about wisdom this week?

Open with prayer and then quote lesson aim. Point out again how important it is to know what the scripture teach about any subject before we start talking about it.

I. What does the scripture say? (Lay down a biblical base for discussion and later decisions.)

Ask: "Which fear listed in the text for today did you find interesting?" (Discuss a little.)

*Ask: "Just for fun, I found another one. What do you think this fear is about?"

Ask: "What were some of the fears the exiles had to deal with?" (List on chalkboard or paper.)

Ask: "Read the second paragraph on page (136). How does the body deal with fear?"

**Ask: "If you had been one of the exiles, what other fears might you have had to deal with?"

Ask: "Our text tells Nehemiah had a plan for rebuilding the city. Where did he start?" (Walls.)

Ask: "How important was Nehemiah's plan for calming the exiles fear?" (Calmed their fears.)

Summary: "Remember from our lesson on David's fight with Goliath what he brought from within himself that took away his fear? (See lesson 2.) If we really believe God is omnipotent, omniscient and omnipresent than we must trust his will for our daily life. It is so easy to ask for help, and then when the fear comes deny him our trust?"

II. How can we apply this great Bible passage to our life today?

Ask: "Many said to their children, 'Don't be afraid.' Was the child's fear realistic? Why?"

Ask: "The author lists his marriage fears and resources on page (139). Where was his help?"

Ask: "Question #1 under Personal Growth asks about self-confidence. Did you find someone?"

Ask: "What does the author believe is one key to successful living?" (Planning (144).

Ask: "How does prioritizing your day help deal with unknown fears?" (Plan your work…)

Ask: "So, what keeps us from asking the Lord for guidance each day and do things His way?"

Summary: "We just can't do it without the Lord providing the courage, strength, and resource."

III. Where is my challenge to serve and how have I answered?

State: "Start this week recording in a journal your fears and how you dealt with them."

Remind your class of the lesson aim and close in prayer.

TEACHING PROCEDURES

CHAPTER 10: ELISHA SAID TO THE PROPHET'S WIFE

Lesson aim: Are you mentoring someone? (Write aim on shelf/butcher paper or chalk board.)

Text: 2 Kings 4:1–7 Additional scripture: Acts 11:26, 13:1–3, Acts 18:26, 1 Corinthians 16:12

Preparation: A teacher's goal: Feed me, teach me to feed myself, and then teach me to feed others. Think about those who have mentored you and gave of their time and resources?

TEACHING OUTLINE:

Review: Did anyone start a journal or write down their plans for the week and then the results? Open with prayer and then quote lesson aim. Point out again how important it is to know what the scripture teaches us about any subject before we start talking about it.

I. What does the scripture say? (Lay down a biblical base for discussion and later decisions.)

Ask: "Let's list reasons why it is important to remember those who helped us along the way!"

Ask: "What was the widow's problem? To whom did she go for help? What did He say?"

Ask: "What did she do that made her happy? What was she supposed to with the left over oil?"

Ask: "Our author asks, 'Would God have filled all the pots and pans?' What do you think?"

Ask: "How important was her faith in communicating to her the sons their need to be obedient?"

Summary: "This is a marvelous story of God's provision and the widow's obedience. How important was obedience for people of the Bible? Is it not just as important for us today?"

II. How can we apply this great Bible passage to our life today?

Ask: "Is there a story you want to tell about how a need was met by someone who cared?"

Ask: "When Christians talk about God's work in the world, what might unbelievers hear?"

(Ego, bragging, humility, joy, faith, trust, doubt, etc.) Which are they likely to believe?"

Ask: "What do you think we need to add to the right words to help unbelievers believe us?"

Ask: "How natural is it for us to do a poor job when it is something we do not want to do?"

Ask: "How do we feel when those on the receiving end realize we didn't care?" (Sorry.)

Ask: "How important is the Golden Rule when we do something for others?"

Ask: "How important is a positive attitude in your work, church, or home? Give an example?"

Summary: "What could happen if every Christian took the Golden Rule seriously and tried to mentor or help one or two people every day? We could change the world couldn't we?"

III. Where is my challenge to serve and how have I answered?

Ask: Add a page or two in your journal this week listing occasions when you tried to do a good deed for someone else. Record your feelings and your thoughts about theirs. Be prepared to share one story next week with our class.

Remind your class of the lesson aim and close in prayer.

TEACHING PROCEDURES

CHAPTER 11: RUTH SAID TO NAOMI

Lesson aim: How to build relationships! (Write aim on shelf/butcher paper or chalk board.)

Text: Ruth 1:16 Additional scripture: Matthew 12:50, Romans 8:17, Ephesians 2:19

Preparation: Ask key church leaders how your church helps mend broken relationships.

TEACHING OUTLINE:

Review: Does anyone have something to share with us from their journal about helping others?

Open with prayer and then quote lesson aim. Point out again how important it is to know what the scripture teaches us about any subject before we start talking about it.

I. What does the scripture say? (Lay down a biblical base for discussion and later decisions.)

Ask: "What was the crisis that brought Ruth and Naomi together heading for Bethlehem?"

Ask: "What rules and cultural traditions did Naomi face?" (Poverty and no family in Moab.)

Ask: "Compare the attitudes of Ruth and Naomi. Were relationships good at the start?"

Ask: "Who will read Ruth's words for us from Ruth 1:15–17? How committed was she?"

Ask: "What did Ruth do to show not only did she love Naomi, she would be there for her?"

Ask: "How did Naomi's life turn out? How did she help Ruth? What is her new job in 4:13–17?"

Summary: "Right words followed by right action build solid relationships. People hear what you say and they see what you do, but when you say it and do it then they know you mean it."

II. How can we apply this great Bible passage to our life today?

Ask: "Who has a story, without names, of a gift you received from someone who didn't care?"

Ask: "How important are good relationships in

our daily life? Do people really care anymore?" Ask: "Find the story about the Dr. and the seminary students. What happens to our brains when in a poor relationships? Name a way we can use spiritual relationships to build our minds?" (Group Bible study, visitation, group prayer meetings, teaching a class, singing in the choir.)

Ask: "What do you think is the cause of so many broken relationships? It is not an easy answer, but one key factor is that the relationship was broken by poor words and poorer actions."

Ask: "What does wealth and fame have to do with broken relationships?" (Ego and selfishness.)

Ask: "What role models today speak exemplary of good marriages and solid relationships?"

Ask: "Did anyone think about an answer to question #1 under Personal Growth?" (Discuss.)

Summary: As Christians we should always help ourselves and others grow spiritually.

III. Where is my challenge to serve and how have I answered?

State: Make list of your current friends/acquaintances, then prioritize the list. Study the list for those with whom you need to spend more time for building a spiritual relationship.

Remind your class of the lesson aim and close in prayer.

TEACHING PROCEDURES

CHAPTER 12: JONATHAN SAID TO DAVID

Lesson aim: Build lasting friendships. (Write aim on shelf/butcher paper or chalk board.)

Text: 1 Samuel 20:42 Additional scripture: Proverbs 17:17, 27:17, John 15:13, 15.

Preparation: Ask class to bring a picture of a childhood friend for show and tell. Look up on the Internet or in a Bible dictionary the word covenant. Be prepared to share in class. (*)

TEACHING OUTLINE:

Review: Did anyone spend some time going over their list of friends this week?

Open with prayer and then quote lesson aim. Point out again how important it is to know what the scripture teaches us about any subject before we start talking about it.

I. What does the scripture say? (Lay down a biblical base for discussion and later decisions.)

Ask: "Show and Tell. Even if you didn't bring a picture tell us about a childhood friend."

State: "Some friendships come and go and some change as we grow older. What changes?"

*Ask: "Can anyone tell us what covenants were like in the Old Testament?"

Ask: "What did the covenant between Jonathan and David's mean to each them?"

Ask: "What were some of the costs involved in their covenant and friendship?"

Ask: "What kind of integrity, honesty, and commitment is found in their covenant?"

Summary: "Covenants are built upon strong relationships and deep commitments. Sometimes there are costs involved when they are broken. Friendships like a marriage can be a covenant."

II. How can we apply this great Bible passage to our life today?

State: "Is the author's definition of friends and acquaintances near or like yours?" (Discuss.)

Ask: "In your opinion is a "spiritual bond" deep/stronger than a friendship? Why or why not?"

Ask: "List some good and bad words that describe many friendships today?" (Self-sacrifice, trust, openness, honesty, caring, motivating, unhealthy, abusive, self-serving, and growing.)

Ask: "How does the meaning of words make a difference between friends?" (Give an example.)

Ask: "What feelings/emotions occur when you end or move a friendship to a lower level?"

Ask: "What might cause you to end or move a friendship to a lower level?"

Summary: "Because we interpret or perceive life differently it may be difficult to maintain or strengthen a friendship. Sometimes it is good to define or clarify in the beginning what your words mean and expectations so it eliminates possible controversy/difficulties down the road."

III. Where is my challenge to serve and how have I answered?

Ask: "Question #1 under the Personal Growth section may be a good exercise to try if you wanted to find or build up a relationship."

Remind your class of the lesson aim and close in prayer.

TEACHING PROCEDURES

CHAPTER 13: ABIGAIL SAID TO DAVID

Lesson aim: Learn how to forgive others. (Write aim on shelf/butcher paper or chalk board.)

Text: 1 Samuel 25:24 Additional scripture: Matthew 6:14–15, Luke 17:4, Acts 13:38

Preparation: Think about your own struggle to practice and deal with forgiveness. Pray for your class that they will learn from this lesson and make forgiving others a real part of their life.

Teaching Outline:

Review: Did anyone do the suggested friends/acquaintance exercise? Did you list forgiveness in the column on characteristics you like in a friend? Is it absent in the acquaintance column?

Open with prayer and then quote lesson aim. Point out again how important it is to know what the scripture teaches us about any subject before we start talking about it.

I. What does the scripture say? (Lay down a biblical base for discussion and later decisions.)

Ask: "What happened in our text for today that made Nabal lose his temper and later his life?"

Ask: "What three things did Abigail do?" (Took food, made a personal visit, ask forgiveness.)

Ask: "What happened the next day when she told Nabal what she had done?" (Heart attack.)

Ask: "What surprise did Abigail have after Nabal died?" (David proposed marriage to her.)

Ask: "Can we assume that God will strike all people who behave like Nabal dead?"

Ask: "What might have happened if Abigail had waited until David and his men arrived?"

Summary: "This Old Testament story shows us the extremes in human behavior. Nabal's words were overruled his brain and it cost him his life. Abigail's words spared his family and servants."

II. How can we apply this great Bible passage to our life today?

Ask: "Is it fair to say that most of us have also made Nabal's mistake?" (Author's tree cutting.)

Ask: "Is it as easy for you as it was for David to change when someone asks for forgiveness?"

Ask: "Is it just as easy to say you are sorry and ask for forgiveness when you don't mean it?"

Ask: "Is discernment a good thing, why don't more people learn or acquire it?" (It takes time.)

Ask: "What does Jesus have to say to us in the Lord's Prayer about forgiveness?"

Ask: "If we seek the truth and try to live by it, will we make Nabal's mistake?" (Less likely.)

Ask: "Name some good things that could happen in your family, church, or community if forgiveness were genuinely practiced?" (Most conflict and heartache would be eliminated)

Summary: "Forgiving others is so easy to say and talk about but so hard to do. Remember it is the right words as well as the right actions that make forgiveness possible."

III. Where is my challenge to serve and how have I answered?

Ask: "Is there a situation or a person who needs to hear or receive your forgiveness soon?"

Remind your class of the lesson aim and close in prayer.

TEACHING PROCEDURES

CHAPTER 14:DAVID SAID TO MEPHIBOSHETH

Lesson aim: How to identify kindness. (Write aim on shelf/butcher paper or chalk board.)

Text: 2 Samuel 9:7 Additional scripture: Romans 12:10–21, Ephesians 4:32, 2 Peter 1:5:-7(*).

Preparation: Cut out a few newspaper stories about kindness for your class. Ask them to identify the kind act. Look for other attitudes mixed with kindness. Discuss these with your class (**).

TEACHING OUTLINE:

Review: "Did you do some evaluation concerning your forgiveness? What did you discover?"

Open with prayer and then quote lesson aim. Point out again how important it is to know what the scripture teaches us about any subject before we start talking about it.

I. What does the scripture say? (Lay down a biblical base for discussion and later decisions.)

Ask: "This lesson picks up on our last two lessons. What did David ask concerning Saul?"

Ask: "What is the difference between David's and Ziba's view of kindness?" (See text)

Ask: "What is your best guess as to how Mephibosheth might view these events?"

*State: "Here are a few New Testament verses to add to our thinking about kindness."

Summary: "Kindness is certainly a Bible trait for

Christians to practice. David goes a long way back to a covenant with Jonathan. Now he can assure Jonathan's son that it is still working."

II. How can we apply this great Bible passage to our life today?

Ask: "What are some mistaken ideas about how we can misinterpret kindness?" (If you give me what I want, or do it for me, always praise me when I show it, and we can always expect it.)

Ask: "David's kindness upset Ziba. Today would this normal or unacceptable behavior?"

Ask: "Our text mentions there is a lot of ambiguity about word meanings. Give us an example."

Ask: "What does the author mean by the dangers of living in a "closed or open system." (214-215)

Ask: "Do you agree with the author that all kindness may not be altruistic?"

Ask: "How much do you think our ego stands in the way of exercising our kindness?"

**Ask: "I have newspaper stories of kindness. Work together to find examples of kindness."

Summary: "Kindness can be expressed in so many ways. Sometimes it is not what you do, but the fact that you show up, support with prayer, or ask the right questions that make it a kind expression of love, hope, and friendship."

III. Where is my challenge to serve and how have I answered?

Ask: "Write down in your journal acts of kindness that were given to you or someone you love."

Remind your class of the lesson aim and close in prayer.

TEACHING PROCEDURES

CHAPTER 15: QUEEN OF SHEBA SAID TO SOLOMON

Lesson aim: Seek a humble spirit (Write aim on shelf/ butcher paper or chalk board.)

Text: 1 Kings 10:7 Additional scripture: Proverbs 16:19, 29:23, Matthew 18:4, James 4:10

Preparation: Find a couple of good articles about humility. Is this a word used only in a spiritual context or are there occasions that it is used in a secular way to describe people. Look for information you can share with your class. (*) Pass out an evaluation sheet.

TEACHING OUTLINE:

Review: Did anyone record acts of kindness in their journal?

Open with prayer and then quote lesson aim. Point out again how important it is to know what the scripture teaches us about any subject before we start talking about it.

I. What does the scripture say? (Lay down a biblical base for discussion and later decisions.)

Ask: "Where made the Queen of Sheba eager to make this journey to see Solomon?"

Ask: "Where did the Queen of Sheba come from and what was her purpose in coming?"

Ask: "Why did she bring gifts? Do you think it was to impress him, humble him or both?"

Ask: "How well did Solomon do in answering her questions? Was she impressed?"

Ask: "Was the Queen surprised? What did she say about him and his servants?" (Verses 7–8.)

Ask: "How does the Queen explain to Solomon that he is blessed?" (I Kings 10:9.)

Summary: "Like the Queen of Sheba most of us are impressed with people who show wisdom, grace and humility. Not everyone can do this, but it is a universal way to find acceptance."

II. How can we apply this great Bible passage to our life today?

Ask: "Can anyone share a story where you tried to impress someone and failed?"

Ask: "How does wealth, good or bad, play a role in our relationships and activities?"

Ask: "Our author says, 'One's spirituality and relationship to God can help make a difficult situation pleasant.' Do you think this is true? If so why or why not?"

Ask: "How important, for you, is humility in selecting potential pastor, leader, or friend?"

Ask: "Are listening or speaking skills more important for you when accepting a new leader."

Ask: "How important is 'star status' for most of us? (Author's comment about Paul Stookey.)

Ask: "What non-verbal cues tell you someone's humility is not real?"

Summary: "Genuine humility is a rare gift from God. However, we can learn its attributes."

III. Where is my challenge to serve and how have I answered?

Ask: "Write down characteristics you think express true humility, and then focus on areas where you are weak and need help. If you are not succeeding find a friend and work together."

Remind your class of the lesson aim, hand out evaluation sheet and close in prayer.

END OF CLASS EVALUATION

These five short questions will help us determine how we can improve the next class. Honesty is important. Please do not put your name on the sheet. Use a 1–10 scale with a 1 as a low score and a 10 as high.

1. Was the classroom comfortable and conducive to a good learning environment? _____

2. Was the text appropriate for your needs and goals for this class? _____

3. Did the questions at the end of each chapter and in class challenge you? _____

4. Did you read and study the text so you were comfortable participating? _____

5. Did you find sufficient helps to change your lifestyle if you choose to do so? _____

SCRIPTURE INDEX

SUBJECT AND AUTHOR INDEX